KS3 English covered — one week at a time!

When it comes to Year 7 English, nothing beats practice — and these CGP 10-Minute Workouts are ideal for short, regular bursts of English.

Every workout covers Reading, Writing and SPaG skills, with a variety of texts to put you to the test. Plus, there's one for each week of the school year — amazing!

Answers are included at the back, along with a handy score sheet to track your progress throughout the year. With CGP, you're onto a winner!

A note for teachers, parents and caregivers

Just something to bear in mind if you're choosing further reading for Year 7 pupils — all the extracts in this book are suitable for children of this age, but we can't vouch for the full texts they're taken from, or other works by the same authors.

Published by CGP
ISBN: 978 1 83774 048 2

Editors: Claire Boulter, Heather Cowley, Robbie Driscoll, Rebecca Greaves, James Summersgill, Kirsty Sweetman

With thanks to Andy Cashmore and John Sanders for the proofreading.

With thanks to Jade Sim for the copyright research.

Clipart from Corel®

Printed by W&G Baird Ltd, Antrim.
Based on the classic CGP style created by Richard Parsons.

Text, design, layout and original illustrations
© Coordination Group Publications Ltd. (CGP) 2023
All rights reserved.

**Photocopying this book is not permitted, even if you have a CLA licence.
Extra copies are available from CGP with next day delivery • 0800 1712 712 • www.cgpbooks.co.uk**

How to Use this Book

- This book contains 36 workouts. We've split them into 3 sections — one for each term, with 12 workouts each. There's roughly one workout for every week of the school year.

- Each workout is out of 12 marks and should take about 10 minutes to complete.

- The workouts start with a short warm-up question, followed by a text with some reading questions. Pupils then move on to a spelling, punctuation or grammar question and finish with some writing skills practice.

- The first 3 workouts are at Year 6 level — they're ideal for reminding pupils of the skills they've learnt in the previous year. These workouts should be done at the start of Year 7.

- The rest of the workouts progress in difficulty, so they're perfect for ensuring that pupils are getting to grips with Year 7 English.

- Answers, a glossary and a score sheet can be found at the back of the book.

The contents page for each term shows you the main reading and writing skills and text types covered in each workout.

Some of these topics are then retested in the following terms at a slightly higher level to provide more practice.

Each workout also tests a different spelling, punctuation or grammar skill, providing practice of a range of topics across the book.

The workouts in each term can be done in any order — pick the one that best suits the needs of your pupils.

The tick boxes on the contents pages can help you to keep a record of which workouts have been attempted.

Contents — Autumn Term

- ☑ **Workout 1** 2
  - Recap of Year 6 Material — Fiction
- ☑ **Workout 2** 4
  - Recap of Year 6 Material — Non-Fiction
- ☑ **Workout 3** 6
  - Recap of Year 6 Material — Poetry
- ☑ **Workout 4** 8
  - Reading Non-Fiction: Identifying Types of Text
  - Writing Non-Fiction: Structuring Your Writing
- ☑ **Workout 5** 10
  - Reading Poetry: Different Types of Poem
  - Writing Poetry: Acrostic Poems
- ☑ **Workout 6** 12
  - Reading Non-Fiction: Finding the Important Bits
  - Writing Non-Fiction: Planning
- ☑ **Workout 7** 14
  - Reading Fiction: Working Out What's Going On
  - Writing Fiction: Structure
- ☑ **Workout 8** 16
  - Reading Non-Fiction: Audience
  - Writing Non-Fiction: Writing to Advise
- ☑ **Workout 9** 18
  - Reading Drama: Summarising
  - Writing Drama: Play Scripts
- ☑ **Workout 10** 20
  - Reading Non-Fiction: Purpose
  - Writing Non-Fiction: Using Paragraphs
- ☑ **Workout 11** 22
  - Reading Poetry: Working Out What's Going On
  - Writing Poetry: Rhyming Couplets
- ☑ **Workout 12** 24
  - Reading Fiction: Language Techniques
  - Writing Fiction: Imagery

Contents — Autumn Term

- [✓] **Workout 1** 2
    - Recap of Year 6 Material — Fiction
- [✓] **Workout 2** 4
    - Recap of Year 6 Material — Non-Fiction
- [✓] **Workout 3** 6
    - Recap of Year 6 Material — Poetry
- [✓] **Workout 4** 8
    - Reading Non-Fiction: Identifying Types of Text
    - Writing Non-Fiction: Structuring Your Writing
- [✓] **Workout 5** 10
    - Reading Poetry: Different Types of Poem
    - Writing Poetry: Acrostic Poems
- [✓] **Workout 6** 12
    - Reading Non-Fiction: Finding the Important Bits
    - Writing Non-Fiction: Planning
- [✓] **Workout 7** 14
    - Reading Fiction: Working Out What's Going On
    - Writing Fiction: Structure
- [✓] **Workout 8** 16
    - Reading Non-Fiction: Audience
    - Writing Non-Fiction: Writing to Advise
- [✓] **Workout 9** 18
    - Reading Drama: Summarising
    - Writing Drama: Play Scripts
- [✓] **Workout 10** 20
    - Reading Non-Fiction: Purpose
    - Writing Non-Fiction: Using Paragraphs
- [✓] **Workout 11** 22
    - Reading Poetry: Working Out What's Going On
    - Writing Poetry: Rhyming Couplets
- [✓] **Workout 12** 24
    - Reading Fiction: Language Techniques
    - Writing Fiction: Imagery

Contents — Spring Term

☑ **Workout 1** 26
- Reading Non-Fiction: Layout and Structure
- Writing Non-Fiction: Writing to Inform, Explain and Advise

☑ **Workout 2** 28
- Reading Fiction: Understanding Characters
- Writing Fiction: Building Character

☑ **Workout 3** 30
- Reading Non-Fiction: Summarising
- Writing Non-Fiction: Redrafting and Proofreading

☑ **Workout 4** 32
- Reading Poetry: Themes
- Writing Poetry: Making Your Writing More Interesting

☑ **Workout 5** 34
- Reading Fiction: Structure
- Writing Fiction: Planning and Writing

☑ **Workout 6** 36
- Reading Non-Fiction: Working Out What's Going On
- Writing Non-Fiction: Essays

☑ **Workout 7** 38
- Reading Drama: Interpreting Plays
- Writing Drama: Using Different Words

☑ **Workout 8** 40
- Reading Non-Fiction: Language Techniques
- Writing Non-Fiction: Writing to Persuade

☑ **Workout 9** 42
- Reading Poetry: Voice
- Writing Poetry: Tone

☑ **Workout 10** 44
- Reading Fiction: What You Think
- Writing Fiction: Using Paragraphs

☑ **Workout 11** 46
- Reading Non-Fiction: Comparing Texts
- Writing Non-Fiction: Writing to Inform, Explain and Advise

☑ **Workout 12** 48
- Reading Fiction: Understanding Setting
- Writing Fiction: Building Setting

Contents — Summer Term

☑ **Workout 1** 50
- Reading Non-Fiction: Layout and Structure
- Writing Non-Fiction: Structure and Planning

☑ **Workout 2** 52
- Reading Poetry: Working Out What's Going On
- Writing Poetry: Tenses

☑ **Workout 3** 54
- Reading Fiction: Context
- Writing Fiction: Redrafting and Proofreading

☑ **Workout 4** 56
- Reading Non-Fiction: What You Think
- Writing Non-Fiction: Writing to Persuade and Argue

☑ **Workout 5** 58
- Reading Drama: Staging and Performance
- Writing Drama: Play Scripts

☑ **Workout 6** 60
- Reading Non-Fiction: Author's Intentions
- Writing Non-Fiction: Using Different Words

☑ **Workout 7** 62
- Reading Poetry: Language Techniques
- Writing Poetry: Language Techniques

☑ **Workout 8** 64
- Reading Fiction: Themes
- Writing Fiction: Structure

☑ **Workout 9** 66
- Reading Non-Fiction: Tone
- Writing Non-Fiction: Formal and Informal Language

☑ **Workout 10** 68
- Reading Fiction: Comparing Texts
- Writing Fiction: Redrafting and Proofreading

☑ **Workout 11** 70
- Reading Non-Fiction: Language Techniques
- Writing Non-Fiction: Essays

☑ **Workout 12** 72
- Reading Poetry: Structure
- Writing Poetry: Different Perspectives

Answers 74

Glossary & Score Sheet 83

Autumn Term: Workout 1

> **Warm up**
>
> 1. Circle the adjective in the sentence below.
>
>   Speaking quietly, the instructor told Monique that she was a capable pilot.
>
>   *(1 mark)*

Reading Questions

> For as long as she could remember, Monique had been obsessed with flying. When she thought about lifting off the ground, a bubble of elation formed in her stomach. When she pictured soaring like an eagle high above the ocean, the bubble exploded like a firework, making her heart race with joy.
>
> Now, finally, she was in the air. From the cockpit, surrounded by the candy floss clouds, she felt herself relax into the seat in which she belonged.

2. Tick the option below that is closest in meaning to "elation".

   victory ☐   excitement ☐   anxiety ☐   pride ☐

   (1 mark)

3. What does the word "obsessed" suggest about Monique's feelings towards flying?

   ....

   (1 mark)

4. What does Monique compare flying to? Copy the quote.

   ....

   (1 mark)

5. How does Monique feel about flying in the second paragraph?
   Use a quote from the text to explain your answer.

   ....

   ....

   ....

   (2 marks)

Spelling, Punctuation & Grammar Question

6. Here's another part of the text. Read it, then underline the spelling mistakes.

> Monique pressed firmly on the ignision and felt the powerfull throb of the engines as they coughed once and then roared into deafening life. As they settled to a gentle rumble, she felt the rythm of her heart slow to a steady beat.

(3 marks)

Writing Question

7. Rewrite the passage below so that it's more interesting. You could add imagery, use adjectives and adverbs, or change the verbs you use.

> The control tower gave Monique permission to take off. She pushed the throttle forwards. The plane started to move along the runway. It moved faster and faster. Monique was very pleased that she was about to fly a plane.

....

....

....

....

....

....

....

....

(3 marks)

Score: /12

Autumn Term: Workout 2

> **Warm up**
>
> 1. Circle the correct spellings of the words below.
>
>   fortunate / fortuneate   historical / historicle   finantial / financial
>
>   *(1 mark)*

Reading Questions

> Over the years, you may well have put loose change into a piggy bank, but have you ever questioned how this receptacle got its name?
>
> The term dates back more than 600 years to the Middle Ages, when it was common practice to store money in jars made from clay known as 'pygg'. These vessels were referred to as 'pygg pots'. Over time, potters with a taste for puns began shaping their clay jars into pigs, and so the modern piggy bank was born.

2. Tick the option below that is closest in meaning to "receptacle".

   utensil ☐   carton ☐   package ☐   container ☐

   (1 mark)

3. According to the text, how long ago were the Middle Ages?

   ....

   (1 mark)

4. What do you think the phrase "common practice" means?

   ....

   (1 mark)

5. According to the text, why did potters begin shaping their pots into pigs?

   ....

   ....

   (1 mark)

Spelling, Punctuation & Grammar Question

6. Here's another part of the text, but it's missing four commas.
   Add the commas in the correct places.

   > However the pig is not the only animal associated with money. In Japanese culture cats are believed to bring prosperity. Many Japanese businesses display a 'Beckoning Cat' statue — a raised right paw attracts money whereas a raised left paw attracts customers. Beckoning Cats have found their way into cartoons art and fashion.

   (4 marks)

Writing Question

7. Rewrite this part of the passage using more formal language.

   > In Chinese culture, people reckon that goldfish bring wealth — it's a belief that's been around for donkey's years. It all started cos the Chinese words for "fish" and "wealth" sound similar.

   ....
   ....
   ....
   ....
   ....
   ....
   ....

   (3 marks)

   Score: /12

Autumn Term: Workout 3

Warm up

1. Which term refers to how beats are arranged in a line of poetry? Tick a box.

    syllable ☐   rhyme scheme ☐   rhythm ☐

    (1 mark)

Reading Questions

> On soft, balmy evenings by the riverside
> Where fireflies flicker and flash,
> As you lean idly back on the grass,
> You may hear a delicate splash.
>
> With sleek head peeking from murky depths
> It isn't that easy to spot her
> But if you are silent and still as a rock
> You may catch a glimpse of an otter.

2. What does the phrase "delicate splash" suggest about how the otter moves?

    ....

    (1 mark)

3. Tick the option below that is closest in meaning to "murky".

    gloomy ☐   bright ☐   dangerous ☐   shady ☐

    (1 mark)

4. What does the poem suggest you do to increase your chance of seeing an otter?

    ....

    (1 mark)

5. What impression do you get of the evenings described?
   Use a quote from the text to explain your answer.

    ....

    ....

    (2 marks)

Spelling, Punctuation & Grammar Question

6. Here's another part of the poem. Read it, then underline the verbs.

   As you wait mutely with eager eyes
   Her suspicion turns to boldness
   She glides across to the riverbank
   And emerges from water's coldness.

   As droplets shimmer on her coat,
   She trots through the golden light
   To a hole beneath a willow tree
   Where she disappears from sight.

   (2 marks)

Writing Question

7. Read the lines below, which are from a different poem. Turn each line into a rhyming couplet by writing a second line which rhymes with the first.

   Through the dark forest the russet fox does stalk

   ....

   The leaves rustle softly in the gathering breeze

   ....

   Silence surrounds me like a golden sphere

   ....

   The liquid trill of a blackbird pierces the hush

   ....

   (4 marks)

   Score: /12

Autumn Term: Workout 4

Warm up

1. Which of the following is **not** a non-fiction text type? Circle your answer.

   | newspaper article | short story | advert | report |

   (1 mark)

Reading Questions

> Hi Mara,
>
> Well, I finally made it to Chile — what an incredible country! I landed in Santiago last week after a pretty tedious flight (but you know me, I get bored if I have to sit still for more than 5 minutes!). I've spent most of my time so far wandering round the city admiring the architecture and sampling the local cuisine, which is divine.
>
> Tomorrow, I head north to the Atacama Desert. I'll need to take plenty of water, as apparently it's one of the driest places in the world. Weirdly, penguins live along the desert coast — fingers crossed I'll get to see them!
>
> Best wishes,
> Ross

2. What type of text is the extract above from? How can you tell?

   ....
   (1 mark)

3. Is the text written in a formal or an informal style?

   ....
   (1 mark)

4. Tick a box to show whether each sentence is a fact or an opinion.

	Fact	Opinion
a) Chile is an incredible country.	☐	☐
b) The local cuisine is delicious.	☐	☐
c) There are penguins in the Atacama Desert.	☐	☐

   (3 marks)

Spelling, Punctuation & Grammar Question

5. Here are some sentences from a travel guide. Underline the spelling mistake in each one, then write the correct spelling on the line.

   a) The mine gives a fascinating glimse into Chile's heritage. ....

   b) Little vegetation thrives in this extremely arid enviroment. ....

   c) Temperatures fall in autum but the weather is still pleasant. ....

   (3 marks)

Writing Question

6. Imagine you're writing an article for a travel guide about somewhere you'd like to go on holiday. Write down five points you'd like to mention, then number them in the boxes to show which order you plan to cover them. You could include points about:

   | where you want to go | why you want to go there | what there is to do |

   .... ☐

   .... ☐

   .... ☐

   .... ☐

   .... ☐

   (3 marks)

Score: ☐ /12

Autumn Term: Workout 5

> **Warm up**
>
> 1. What name is given to poems that don't rhyme or have a regular rhythm? Tick a box.
>
>   free verse ☐   loose verse ☐   open verse ☐
>
>   *(1 mark)*

Reading Questions

> Baking a Poem
>
> Ideas race to the front of my mind,
> Ingredients for a new recipe.
> Measuring out each word I find,
> They spill from my pen steadily.
>
> Into the mix, I fold a rhyme,
> To keep it fluffy and light.
> Then add rhythm, to keep the time,
> And sprinkle similes from a height.
>
> The page now full — it's time to proof.
> I knead my words: reassess, rephrase.
> The sounds satisfy my sweetest tooth;
> I cast a smile pagewards in praise.
>
> Like baking bread, I see the words rise.
> They nourish my heart, a spiritual prize.

2. What type of poem is this? Tick a box.

   haiku ☐   limerick ☐   ballad ☐   sonnet ☐

   (1 mark)

3. The words "spill" from the narrator's pen. What does this suggest?

   ....

   (1 mark)

4. Find two quotes which show that the narrator is proud of their poem.

   ....

   ....

   (2 marks)

Spelling, Punctuation & Grammar Question

5. Complete these sentences by circling the correct preposition.

   a) Pass the flour **through / beneath** a sieve to eliminate any lumps.

   b) Soften the block of butter **into / in** the microwave.

   c) All the bakers **except / despite** Shelley were extremely nervous.

   d) The showstopping cake was created **from / by** the master baker.

   (4 marks)

Writing Question

6. In an acrostic poem, the first letters of each line combine to spell out a word or phrase. Look at this example:

   Encased in a hard brown shell.
   Golden-centred and runny.
   Great for cakes and puddings.

   Write an acrostic poem for the word 'baking'.

   B ....
   A ....
   K ....
   I ....
   N ....
   G ....

   (3 marks)

   Score: /12

Autumn Term: Workout 6

Warm up

1. Which of the following would you **not** find in a news report? Circle your answer.

   headline   slogan   quotes   facts

   (1 mark)

Reading Questions

LOCAL GROUP SET TO MAKE A SPLASH AT ROCKSTEADY

This weekend, a group of Guardwell lifeguards hopes to continue their success on the UK music scene. The lifeguards, collectively known as *The Ocean Drops*, are due to play their first live set in front of a crowd of thousands at the world-famous Rocksteady Festival near Leightonchester.

The Ocean Drops met at a first aid course last year. Recounting the group's origins, lead singer Aliana told the *Guardwell Gazette*, "It was a perfect storm — Tom was showing us how chest compressions have the same rhythm as a drum beat, and then, in turn, Mo said that he plays guitar and Aurora said she plays keyboard. That night, we had our first jamming session, and the rest is history."

The group has already had some success, with their debut album *Poolside Paradise* reaching number 84 on the UK album charts. Their sound draws on the catchy 'surf-rock' style made famous by iconic bands such as *The Beach Boys*. *The Ocean Drops*' upbeat songs, as bassist Eddie describes, evoke "the sound of crashing tides and water slides".

2. How soon after they met did *The Ocean Drops* first play together?

   ....

   (1 mark)

3. Tick a box to show whether each statement is true or false.

	True	False
a) Aurora is the band's bass player.	☐	☐
b) The band plays versions of *The Beach Boys*' songs.	☐	☐
c) *Poolside Paradise* is the band's first album.	☐	☐

   (3 marks)

Spelling, Punctuation & Grammar Question

4. Add a pair of brackets to each of the sentences below.

   a) The drummer the musician who started the band uses a variety of instruments to recreate the sound of crashing waves .

   b) There are rumours largely unconfirmed ones that a new album is in the works to capitalise on the success of *Poolside Paradise* .

   (2 marks)

Writing Question

5. Imagine you have been asked to write a review of a band or singer you have listened to recently. In the table below, write a plan for your review that outlines your introduction, three main points and conclusion.

Introduction	
Point 1	
Point 2	
Point 3	
Conclusion	

(5 marks)

Score: ☐ / 12

Autumn Term: Workout 7

Warm up

1. When talking about stories, what is meant by the term 'structure'?

   ....

   (1 mark)

Reading Questions

> There were only two things on my mind: the punch I had just received square on the shoulder, and the grimacing, burly man grinding his teeth on the opposite side of the ring. My lip quivered as I clumsily hauled myself to my knees, and then to my feet.
>
> The referee approached and clasped my helmet. He looked me in the eyes and checked if I was willing to continue. As if possessed by an unseen force, I raised my arms to guard my head and nodded resolutely.

2. What does the phrase "My lip quivered" suggest about how the narrator feels?

   ....

   (1 mark)

3. Circle the correct option to complete each sentence.

   a) The **narrator / opponent** has been knocked down by a punch.

   b) The **referee / opponent** is burly and grimacing.

   c) After getting up, the narrator is feeling **anxious / determined**.

   (3 marks)

4. What does the phrase "As if possessed by an unseen force" suggest about the narrator's actions?

   ....

   ....

   (1 mark)

Spelling, Punctuation & Grammar Question

5. Underline the misspelt word in each sentence.
   Then write the correct spelling on the line.

   a) The audeince cheered after the bell chimed.   ....

   b) Too exhausted, my freind couldn't continue the match.   ....

   c) I beamed as I recieved the championship cup.   ....

   (3 marks)

Writing Question

6. Below are three possible opening sentences of a story about a boxer preparing for an important fight. Tick a box to choose one of the sentences to start your story, then write the rest of the opening paragraph. Think about how to make your writing gripping, so that the reader wants to find out what happens next.

   a) As I leapt into the ring, I fixed my opponent with a confident stare. ☐

   b) My palms sweat inside my gloves as my arms and legs tremble. ☐

   c) I know I can do this. I've beaten him before and I can do it again. ☐

   ....

   ....

   ....

   ....

   ....

   ....

   ....

   ....

   (3 marks)

   Score: ☐ / 12

Autumn Term: Workout 8

> **Warm up**
>
> 1. Draw lines to link each text to its most likely audience.
>
>   a guide on making lesson plans   an MP
>
>   a list of school rules   a pupil
>
>   a report on the UK education system   a teacher
>
>   *(2 marks)*

Reading Questions

> I am writing to inform you that Zene has been selected to receive a prize at our upcoming prize-giving ceremony. She has demonstrated a remarkable talent for the creative arts — we were particularly impressed by her performance in the autumn term musical. Zene is an exemplary pupil of Longleaf High School and we are delighted with her progress this year.
>
> The ceremony will take place in the school hall at 2pm on Friday 18th March, and an afternoon tea reception will follow. Please contact me at pam.greenwood@azmail.co.uk to reserve up to three guest tickets.

2. Who do you think is the audience of this letter?

   ....
   (1 mark)

3. Is this letter formal or informal? Give an example to support your answer.

   ....

   ....
   (2 marks)

Spelling, Punctuation & Grammar Question

4. For each word in bold, decide whether it needs a hyphen. If it does, rewrite it with the hyphen in the correct place. If it doesn't, write 'No hyphen'.

   a) We are impressed with her **selfdiscipline**. ....

   b) The letter never arrived, so the school **resent** it. ....

   c) The cast have been **preoccupied** with the musical. ....

   (3 marks)

Writing Questions

5. Tick the box next to the sentence you would be most likely to include in an email advising a friend about how to play the drums.

   a) Snare, bass and tom-toms are all different types of drum. ☐

   b) My brother played the drums but he had no sense of rhythm. ☐

   c) It's a good idea to set aside a few minutes every day to practise. ☐

   (1 mark)

6. Imagine you're Zene. Write a letter to a friend, advising them about how to prepare for an audition for the next school musical. Start and end your letter appropriately and use informal language.

   ....

   ....

   ....

   ....

   ....

   ....

   ....

   (3 marks)

   Score: ☐ / 12

Autumn Term: Workout 9

> **Warm up**

1. Circle the correct phrase to complete each sentence below.

   When summarising a text, you should write down **every point** / **the key points**.

   In a summary, you should use **your own words** / **the exact words from the text**.

   (2 marks)

Reading Questions

A dusty, dingy attic, crowded with boxes, old pieces of furniture and various other items.
EWAN *and* **ALICE** *emerge through a hatch from below, each holding a torch.*

ALICE *(continuing a conversation)* What are we even looking for? Gran said—

EWAN I know, but come on! This might be our only chance to snoop in her attic.

EWAN *begins noisily rifling through boxes while* **ALICE** *lingers by the hatch uncertainly. Eventually, noticing a small book on a nearby shelf, she picks it up and begins to read it.*

ALICE This is interesting... It's some kind of diary. I think it's Gran's handwriting.

There is the sound of the front door slamming. The children freeze for a moment, then rush for the hatch. In his haste, **EWAN** *knocks over a coat stand, which lands with a thud.*

GRAN *(from below)* Children! What's going on? I do hope you're behaving...

2. Which of the following best summarises the difference between Ewan and Alice? Tick a box.

   Ewan is sensible, whereas Alice is mischievous. ☐

   Ewan is careless, whereas Alice is cautious. ☐

   Ewan is outgoing, whereas Alice is shy. ☐

   (1 mark)

3. Write one sentence that briefly summarises what happens in the extract above.

   ....

   ....

   (2 marks)

Spelling, Punctuation & Grammar Question

4. Rewrite each sentence by replacing the noun in bold with a suitable pronoun.

   a) Alice found **the diary**.   ....

   b) **The siblings** had torches.   ....

   (2 marks)

Writing Questions

5. The extract below shows the next part of the script from page 18, but it is missing stage directions. Add some sensible stage directions in the spaces provided.

   ALICE   (..) What have you done? Let's go!

   EWAN   There's no time — I can hear her footsteps. We'll just have to hide.

   ....

   (2 marks)

6. Imagine that Gran finds Alice and Ewan hiding in the attic.
   Write a few lines of dialogue to show what happens.
   Make it clear who's speaking and add stage directions.

   ....

   ....

   ....

   ....

   ....

   ....

   (3 marks)

Score: /12

Autumn Term: Workout 10

Warm up

1. Draw lines to link each text to its most likely purpose.

   a newspaper article about a famous climber — to advise

   a children's story about a magical journey — to entertain

   a magazine article with tips for buying walking boots — to inform

   (2 marks)

Reading Questions

> Itching to explore New Zealand's stunning scenery, but unsure where to start? With bases in many of the country's most popular national parks, Trailblazer Trekz is in a unique position to turn your dream into reality. Whether you are looking to hike five kilometres or five hundred, our experienced team are guaranteed to guide you somewhere that truly takes your breath away. Maybe you've always wanted to tackle the spectacular Tongariro Alpine Crossing, celebrated as one of the world's best single-day hikes. Or perhaps you've set your sights on a multi-day trek through the majestic glacial valleys and untamed rainforest of the Milford Track. At Trailblazer Trekz, no challenge is too big or too small. Contact us today to find out more.

2. What is the main purpose of the text? Tick one box.

   to explain ☐   to advise ☐   to persuade ☐

   (1 mark)

3. Find a piece of evidence that supports your answer to Q2 and explain how it supports your answer.

   ....

   ....

   (2 marks)

Spelling, Punctuation & Grammar Question

4. Complete these sentences by using the words in brackets to form comparatives.
   You need to decide whether to use 'more' or add the suffix '-er'.

   a) The trail is .... in summer than in winter. *(busy)*

   b) New Zealand is even .... than I expected. *(beautiful)*

   c) The west coast has .... weather than the east. *(wet)*

   (3 marks)

Writing Question

5. a) Read this passage about mountaineering as a hobby. Add appropriate linking words or phrases in the gaps to emphasise that a new point is being made.

   > People take up mountaineering for many reasons. Many are drawn to the sport because it challenges them, both physically and mentally. It appeals precisely because it takes climbers out of their comfort zone.
   >
   > ...., mountaineering gives people the opportunity to enjoy the great outdoors and appreciate the beauty of the natural world. Climbing up to a mountain summit can literally take your breath away.
   >
   > ...., few people realise quite how expensive it is. Aside from all the pricey equipment, would-be mountaineers have to factor in the cost of travel to remote locations and the need for appropriate insurance.

   (2 marks)

   b) Now write the first two sentences of the next paragraph.
      You should begin your paragraph with an appropriate linking phrase.

   ....

   ....

   ....

   (2 marks)

   Score: ☐ / 12

Autumn Term: Workout 11

> **Warm up**
>
> 1. Briefly explain what a rhyme scheme is.
>
>   ....
>
>   *(1 mark)*

Reading Questions

The Trainspotter

In beanie hat and anorak,
With eyes fixed firmly on the track,
He calmly stood on Platform 3,
And waited for trains patiently.

A passer-by who saw him laughed:
"What a loser! He must be daft
To sit and wait for trains all day.
They're all the same anyway."

Pleased with this cruel condemnation,
The passer-by left the station.
At home she finished last night's tea,
And settled down to watch TV.

In woolly socks and comfy jeans,
With eyes fixed firmly on the screen,
She yawned and stretched and lay in wait
To catch the show at half past eight.

2. The trainspotter's eyes are "fixed firmly on the track". What does this mean?

   ....

   (1 mark)

3. Give a quote from the poem that shows the passer-by's opinion of the trainspotter.

   ....

   (1 mark)

4. Explain how the final stanza suggests that the passer-by isn't as different to the trainspotter as she thinks.

   ....

   ....

   ....

   (2 marks)

Spelling, Punctuation & Grammar Question

5. Rewrite the passage below, putting capital letters in the correct places.

   on friday, i took the train to york to see my friend amy. sadly, it was delayed.

   ....

   ....
   (3 marks)

Writing Question

6. Here's the first verse of a poem called 'Ghost Train'.

   In this very spot in bygone years,
   A railway train passed right through here.
   Now those old tracks are the only sign
   That there ever was a railway line.

   a) On the lines below, write down some of your own words or phrases that you'd associate with a ghost train.

   ....

   ....
   (1 mark)

   b) Use some of the words from part a) to help you complete the next verse of the poem. You should use rhyming couplets.

   Except at night, so the story goes,

   ....

   ....

   ....

   (3 marks)

   Score: /12

Autumn Term: Workout 12

Warm up

1. True or false? A simile describes something by saying it is like something else.

   ....
   (1 mark)

Reading Questions

> Later that day, Aisyah decided to swim to the island. Slipping out across the veranda, she crept down to the beach and scrutinised the sea. The horizon was broken only by the dark bulk of the island, which loomed ominously like a crocodile emerging from a swamp. The sky, which in the morning had been clear and blue, had now faded to a pale grey, and an army of dark clouds could be seen to Aisyah's left, threatening to charge inland with the force of the incoming tide.
>
> Still, Aisyah predicted it would be an hour or more until the rain came. And the island was not far. She stepped into the shallows with a soft splash.

2. In the text above, find and copy an example of:

   a) a simile.

   ....

   b) onomatopoeia.

   ....
   (2 marks)

3. The clouds are described as an "army" that is "threatening to charge inland".

   a) What technique is used here?

   ....

   b) Which of the following best describes the mood created by this technique?

   menacing ☐   tranquil ☐   frantic ☐

   (2 marks)

Spelling, Punctuation & Grammar Question

4. Here's another part of the story. Read it, then underline the abstract nouns.

> Filled with excitement, Aisyah glided through the rolling waves. She enjoyed the freedom of being alone in the water and the feeling of her arms and legs working hard to propel herself forwards. Glancing ahead, she saw the island already drawing near. Who knew what mysteries it might hold?

(2 marks)

Writing Questions

5. Write down a suitable metaphor to fill the gap in each sentence below.

   a) Aisyah was a .... in the water.

   b) The waves were .... as they crashed into the shore.

(2 marks)

6. Write a description of what the island is like when Aisyah reaches it. Include one simile and one metaphor. You could think about:

   | what Aisyah can see | what she can hear | how the island makes her feel |

   ....

   ....

   ....

   ....

   ....

   ....

(3 marks)

Score: /12

Spring Term: Workout 1

Warm up

1. Underline the imperatives (command words) in the sentence below.

   Enter the rocket with your crew, fasten your seatbelt and start the engine.

   (1 mark)

Reading Questions

Mini-Earth — Earth's Smaller Sibling

Discovery
Scientist P. Lanesite was behind the shock discovery of Mini-Earth. Other scientists were baffled as to how this Earth-like planet went unnoticed for so long, given it's located within the familiar bounds of our solar system.

Landscape
Mini-Earth's varied terrain includes deserts, jungles and mountain ranges.

Lifeforms
Mini-Earth diverges from Earth in terms of its unusual wildlife, the likes of which have never been seen before.

Location
Mini-Earth is 3.2 billion km from Earth. With our advanced technology, it has taken a rocket only 8 years to reach this planet.

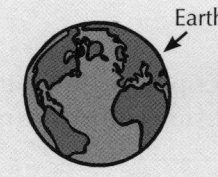

2. Why do you think the writer has used subheadings?

   ....
   (1 mark)

3. How does the diagram help the reader to understand the topic?

   ....
   (1 mark)

4. Why do you think the writer chose to put the 'Discovery' section first?

   ....

   ....
   (1 mark)

Spelling, Punctuation & Grammar Question

5. For each sentence, circle the correct spelling of the word in bold.

   a) The scientists gave us **advice / advise** about travelling to outer space.

   b) Before going to space, you should **practice / practise** being in zero gravity.

   c) The astronaut recently acquired their **licence / license** to fly a spacecraft.

   (3 marks)

Writing Questions

6. Pretend you're an astronaut explaining how to greet an Eary (a dangerous creature on Mini-Earth). Think of two steps to complete these instructions.

   a) Approach the Eary quietly, as this species has sensitive hearing.

   b) ....

   c) ....

   d) Compliment the Eary. Be heartfelt, as they can hear the tremor of a lie.

   (2 marks)

7. Write a short paragraph that informs astronauts from Earth about Mini-Earth's climate and advises them on what clothes and equipment to bring if they visit.

   ....

   ....

   ....

   ....

   ....

   (3 marks)

Score: /12

Spring Term: Workout 2

> **Warm up**
>
> 1. True or false? Reported speech is when you quote the exact words that were spoken.
>
>   ....
>   *(1 mark)*

Reading Questions

> Inspector Ricci strode towards the house and knocked loudly on the front door. Through a small frosted pane, she spied a figure slowly approaching to unlock the door. They opened it only a sliver, peering out with narrowed eyes and bared teeth. Though sweat had erupted on her brow, Inspector Ricci remained composed.
> "I'm looking for a missing goa-," she began.
> But before she could finish, the figure snapped, "It's not here."
> Inspector Ricci bit back the response ready to fire off her tongue. Realising the figure was more an animal than a person, she decided to change her approach, but after uttering only a single sugar-coated syllable, she was interrupted once again.
> "That missing goat's got nothing to do with me, and if you think it does, I dare you to prove it," hissed the figure, before slamming the door in her face.

2. Which adjective best describes Inspector Ricci at the start of the passage?

   troubled ☐   arrogant ☐   confident ☐   curious ☐

   (1 mark)

3. What does the phrase "sugar-coated syllable" suggest about Inspector Ricci's speech?

   ....
   (1 mark)

4. Find and copy one quote that could suggest the figure is guilty of being involved in the goat's disappearance. Explain your answer.

   ....

   ....
   (2 marks)

Spelling, Punctuation & Grammar Question

5. Write 'Yes' or 'No' to show whether each sentence needs inverted commas.

   a) The suspect was uncooperative, Inspector Ricci said to the sheriff.   ....

   b) The sheriff said that we should collect more witness statements.   ....

   c) We told farmers to watch their goats carefully given recent events.   ....

   (3 marks)

Writing Question

6. Write a version of the story on page 28 where the character behind the door is nervous rather than hostile. Think about what they would say, how they would behave and what you could compare them to.

   ....

   ....

   ....

   ....

   ....

   ....

   ....

   ....

   ....

   ....

   ....

   (4 marks)

Score: /12

Spring Term: Workout 3

Warm up

1. Circle the correct option to complete the sentence below.

   The habitat of **them** / **those** sea turtles is in danger and must be protected.

   (1 mark)

Reading Questions

> Dear Kiyana,
>   My summer in Greece is nearly over. It seems like only yesterday that I joined an organisation which cleans up beach habitats and monitors sea turtles as they hatch.
> All I'll say is, it's amazing how much of a difference we've made in only a few months!
>   If you didn't know, sea turtles often fall ill due to ingesting plastic and other rubbish. In addition, their hatching process is harmed by light pollution. After hatching, sea turtles should follow the moonlight to the sea, but they often crawl towards light from buildings instead. By guiding these hatchlings to the sea, we've saved many from becoming lost.
>   Taking part in these activities has been so rewarding, and I even made some friends in the process. Despite it being exhausting at times, I wouldn't change a thing.
> If I've learnt anything, it's that taking action does make a difference.
>   From Pedro

2. Write a few words to summarise:

   a) the first paragraph ....

   b) the second paragraph ....

   (2 marks)

3. Summarise Pedro's feelings about the work he did in Greece.

   ....

   (1 mark)

4. Find and copy a phrase from the third paragraph that sums up the whole text.

   ....

   (1 mark)

Spelling, Punctuation & Grammar Question

5. Write each verb in bold in the simple past tense.

   a) We **pick** up the litter and **throw** it in a bin.   .... / ....

   b) I **get** food for the turtles and **take** it to them.   .... / ....

   (2 marks)

Writing Questions

6. This is Kiyana's response to Pedro, in which she tells him about her summer holiday. Proofread it carefully, then circle each mistake and write the correction above it.

   > Wow, your trip sounds amazeing! I had a similar experience this summer, actually.
   >
   > I desided to volunteer at my local animal shelter, where I helped too take care of many
   >
   > creatures. The kitten's were particularly adorable. However, the lizard (which was very
   >
   > irritable kept scratching me. My kindness didn't seem to effect its mood, but I still tried.

   (3 marks)

7. Redraft this text so it uses more interesting vocabulary and sentence structures.

   > When a sea turtle hatches, it goes into the sea. Then, it finds its way back to the place it was born so it can lay more eggs. When their eggs hatch, the cycle repeats.

   ....

   ....

   ....

   ....

   (2 marks)

Score: / 12

Spring Term: Workout 4

> **Warm up**
>
> 1. What is meant by a text's 'theme'? Circle the correct option.
>
> | the text's main idea | how it makes you feel | the writing style |
>
>   *(1 mark)*

Reading Questions

> Nose down, straight as an arrow,
> We are one, the kayak and I.
> White water, swirls and eddies,
> We battle to stay on course.
> The river's rage surrounds us,
> Forceful fists pummel the paddle,
> Numb my arm, stun my shoulder.
> The paddle's a dead weight
> Dragging me into the torrent.
> The bow starts to dip,
> The stern starts to rise.
> I brace myself.

2. a) Which of the following best describes the poem's narrator? Tick a box.

   They are used to being in a kayak. ☐

   They feel out of place in a kayak. ☐

   b) Explain why you chose this option.

   ....

   (2 marks)

3. One of the themes explored in this poem is the power of nature.
   Find a quote from the poem in which nature appears powerful.

   ....

   (1 mark)

4. Which do you think is portrayed as the more powerful force in the poem, the power of humans or the power of nature? Explain your answer.

   ....

   ....

   (1 mark)

Spelling, Punctuation & Grammar Question

5. Here are some more lines from the same poem. Fill in each gap with the present tense form of the verb in brackets.

    a) I .... like a leaf in a gale. *(to toss)*

    b) Panic nearly .... me. *(to consume)*

    c) The jagged rock .... too fast. *(to approach)*

    (3 marks)

Writing Question

6. Rewrite these lines from the same poem, adding adjectives, adverbs and imagery to make them more interesting and dramatic.

    I paddle hard and miss the rock.

    ....

    I am carried out of the rapids.

    ....

    I float downstream.

    ....

    The water is calm now.

    ....

    (4 marks)

Score: /12

Spring Term: Workout 5

Warm up

1. What does 'chronological' mean?

   ....
   (1 mark)

Reading Questions

> I sat silently in the dressing room, enveloped by my cheering teammates. I was dumbstruck — I couldn't believe I had scored the winner in the Yorkshire Youths final. I closed my eyes and relived the moment again...
>
> I feel the seconds ticking down as Kwame runs up to the corner flag. Both teams are on edge, so there's some apprehensive jostling in the box. Spotting the ball swooping into the box, I jump and head it into the goal. I score! My teammates swarm me. With a grin, I look to my parents in the stands.

2. How can you tell that this text is not written chronologically?

   ....

   ....
   (1 mark)

3. What does the phrase "on edge" suggest about how both teams were feeling?

   ....
   (1 mark)

4. a) Why do you think the narrator sat "silently" in the dressing room?

   ....

   b) Find a quote from the text to support your answer to part a).

   ....
   (2 marks)

Spelling, Punctuation & Grammar Question

5. Circle the misspelt word in each sentence, then write the correct spelling on the line.

    a) Kwame rapidly ran passed the defender. ....

    b) Everyone accept the goalkeeper was in the box. ....

    c) Their was not much time until the final whistle. ....

    (3 marks)

Writing Question

6. Imagine you are writing a story about one of the topics below.

    | a sporting world record that has been broken | a match between humans and aliens | the invention of a new sport |

    a) Make a plan of what will happen in your story.

    Opening: ....

    ....

    Middle: ....

    ....

    Ending: ....

    (2 marks)

    b) Now write the opening of your story below.

    ....

    ....

    ....

    ....

    (2 marks)

    Score: /12

Spring Term: Workout 6

Warm up

1. What is the main difference between an autobiography and a biography?

   ....

   ....
   (1 mark)

Reading Questions

> My earliest memory was seeing the Roman legion marching through my village in the winter of AD 45. I was 2 years old at the time and hadn't recognised the stifling sense of threat that hung heavy in the air. The Romans had invaded much of southern Britain by this point and were showing no sign of stopping. For a time, resistance had been fierce, but it had slowly waned as rebellion after rebellion had been cut down.
>
> Fast forward to my seventeenth birthday, and by that time we had fully "accepted" Roman rule. But on that day, some of the nearby villages had assembled a band of fighters, each one wanting to be rid of the Romans. They intended to launch a series of ambushes on Roman garrisons, and I was tasked with leading them.

2. Is this text written in the first-person or third-person? How can you tell?

   ....
   (1 mark)

3. Find a quote from the text that shows the villagers were sick of Roman rule.

   ....
   (1 mark)

4. What do you notice about the word "accepted" above? Why is it written this way?

   ....

   ....
   (2 marks)

Spelling, Punctuation & Grammar Question

5. Add the suffix to the root word, making spelling changes if they are needed. Write the new word on the line to complete each sentence.

   a) I am not .... *(hope + ful)* that we will win this battle.

   b) I could hear the Romans marching .... *(steady + ly)*.

   c) Then, the marching stopped. It was .... *(strange + ly)* quiet.

   (3 marks)

Writing Question

6. Below is a mind map for an essay titled 'How did the British people resist Roman rule?'. Using the mind map, write an introduction that summarises the main points of the essay.

   British warrior Caratacus defeated Romans in battle — Mid-1st century

   Later in the 1st century

   Picts from Scotland harassed Romans — Resistance to Roman rule — Boudica (Queen of a British tribe) revolted against Romans

   Led to Romans building Hadrian's Wall — Early 2nd century

   ....
   ....
   ....
   ....
   ....
   ....
   ....

   (4 marks)

   Score: /12

Spring Term: Workout 7

> **Warm up**
>
> 1. In a play, what is a monologue?
>
>   ....
>
>   *(1 mark)*

Reading Questions

> *In a dark cabin covered in hanging cobwebs,* **AGGIE** *and* **HILDA** *stand around a bubbling cauldron, the glowing flames flickering various hues of orange over their faces.*
>
> **AGGIE** *(tossing a frog's leg into the cauldron)* Well, that should do it, Hilda!
>
> **HILDA** Mmmm, smells lovely! *(eagerly)* Shall we have a glug now?
>
> **HILDA** *snatches a nearby goblet and plunges it into the swampy broth.*
>
> **AGGIE** No! The prince has paid a pretty penny for this potion of beauty and he'll not be satisfied unless he has every drop. Besides, I can make you a batch later. *(under her breath)* You certainly need it.
>
> **HILDA** I heard that!
>
> **HILDA** *huffs and turns around, accidentally knocking over a glass tube of black liquid. It trickles into the cauldron, creating a small hiss.* **HILDA** *and* **AGGIE** *leave silently.*

2. How can you tell that Hilda is excited to try the potion?

   ....

   (1 mark)

3. Why does Aggie speak her final line "under her breath"?

   ....

   (1 mark)

4. Do you think either witch realised that Hilda knocked the black liquid into the cauldron? Explain your answer using evidence from the text.

   ....

   ....

   (2 marks)

Spelling, Punctuation & Grammar Question

5. These are some instructions from Hilda and Aggie's potion recipe, but they are missing commas. Add in the missing commas in the correct places.

   a) Chop an onion a rat's tail a hemlock root and a piece of bark.

   b) Take the lock of hair tie it into a knot and dip it in the liquid.

   c) Mix in the soot stir once drop in a frog's leg and let it simmer.

   (3 marks)

Writing Question

6. Here is the start of the next scene of the script on the previous page.
   Rewrite it so that it uses more interesting words and phrases.

   > **AGGIE** *and* **HILDA** *are in a nice palace.* **AGGIE** *is clutching a small glass tube under her cloak. The* **PRINCE** *approaches them.*
   >
   > **PRINCE** And so we meet again... *(hushed)* Have you made it?
   >
   > **AGGIE** Of course. *(AGGIE produces the potion)* It's our best one yet.
   >
   > **PRINCE** *(He grabs the potion and drinks it in one gulp.)* Ew! That tastes bad!

   ....

   ....

   ....

   ....

   ....

   ....

   ....

   ....

   ....

   (4 marks)

   Score: /12

Spring Term: Workout 8

Warm up

1. What is the purpose of most advertisements? Tick the correct option.

   to entertain ☐   to advise ☐   to persuade ☐   to argue ☐

   (1 mark)

Reading Questions

Sheepsdale Campsite
Be at one with nature.

Come and visit our beautiful campsite, nestled in the idyllic Cumbrian countryside. Sheepsdale Campsite is ideal for families and friends of any age. We boast the nation's most luxurious tents, which come fully fitted with everything you could need and more. Explore the stunning local area before returning to your tent to float like a cloud on our state-of-the-art, super-soft beds. So what are you waiting for?

Book by 30th August to receive 25% off — visit our website or call 01134 960960.

2. Copy the slogan from the advert above.

   ....
   (1 mark)

3. For each quote from the text, write down whether it contains a simile, a superlative, a command or a rhetorical question.

   a) "Explore the stunning local area"   ....

   b) "We boast the nation's most luxurious tents"   ....

   c) "So what are you waiting for?"   ....

   d) "returning to your tent to float like a cloud" ....

   (4 marks)

Spelling, Punctuation & Grammar Question

4. Complete these sentences using suitable punctuation.

    a) Have you experienced a Sheepsdale Campsite bed yet..........

    b) There are some breathtaking views at Planter's Gorge..........

    c) "Sheepsdale is unbelievable," one customer said. "What a holiday..........

    (3 marks)

Writing Questions

5. Complete this sentence advertising a torch by writing a list of three in the gap.

    The *AlwaysBright* torch is ....

    ....

    (1 mark)

6. Write a paragraph advertising an imaginary piece of camping equipment.
    Convince readers to buy it by providing information about it and using persuasive techniques.

    ....

    ....

    ....

    ....

    ....

    ....

    ....

    ....

    (2 marks)

Score: /12

Spring Term: Workout 9

> **Warm up**
>
> 1. Which type of narration uses the pronoun "you" to speak directly to the reader?
>
>   ....
>
>   *(1 mark)*

Reading Questions

23 Zinnia Lane

It's loneliest at night, or so I've found,
When nothing inside me makes a sound.
My lights are off, my walls are bare,
Nothing disturbs the stagnant air.
I miss the time when my rooms were full;
Now I'm a mere shell, an empty skull.

The silence inside is far too loud,
No echo of a cry, a laugh or shout.
Gone are the sounds that filled this spot.
I hope this is a dream; I know it's not.
But though I've never felt more alone,
I'm glad they could once call me home.

2. Who or what is the narrator of the poem?

   ....

   (1 mark)

3. Why do you think the poet uses the first-person? Circle the correct option.

   | so the reader can understand the narrator's feelings | to give the poem a steady pace |

   (1 mark)

4. a) Think of a word that describes the overall tone of the poem.

   ....

   b) Find and copy three words from the poem that help to create this tone.

   ....

   (2 marks)

Spelling, Punctuation & Grammar Question

5. Here's another part of the poem. Underline the correct spellings.

> I was shelter from the **weather / whether**
> Back when we all lived together.
> They left not a **peace / piece** behind,
> Just memories lingering in my mind.
>
> No matter if they are far or near,
> I will always want them **hear / here**.
> If they kept hold of their old key,
> They can **maybe / may be** visit me.

(4 marks)

Writing Questions

6. The two lines below are a continuation of the poem, but now the tone is excited.
   Write two lines to continue this part of the poem,
   keeping an excited tone and using rhyming couplets.

> Then one bright day, much to my joy,
> In came a family with a young boy!

....

....
(1 mark)

7. Continue the poem by writing four lines of your own using a tone of your choice.
   You don't have to keep the rhyme scheme of the poem.

....

....

....

....
(2 marks)

Score: ☐ / 12

Spring Term: Workout 10

Warm up

1. Give one reason you would start a new paragraph in a story.

   ....
   (1 mark)

Reading Questions

> Keep quiet, play dumb, don't draw attention to yourself. I know the drill by now. After all, this is my third new school in as many months. And OK, so on the surface it seems alright — new computer lab, teachers who smile and know my name, no obvious bullying. I know it's only a matter of time, though, before the 'conversations' start again. "So much <u>potential</u>... If only she'd <u>try</u>... Maybe we're just not the right <u>fit</u> for one another..." And off we go again — so long; auf wiedersehen; sayonara; don't call us, we won't call you...
>
> Trouble is, I do try. And apparently I still don't 'fit', whatever that means. Like I'm a too-small shoe or a T-shirt you've outgrown.

2. Write down three words that describe how the first paragraph makes you feel about the character and her situation.

   ....
   (1 mark)

3. What effect does the use of the first-person have on the reader?

   ....
   (1 mark)

4. a) Circle the word which best describes the narrator of this text.

   | unintelligent | frustrated | bored | mischievous |

   b) Explain why you chose this word.

   ....

   ....
   (2 marks)

Spelling, Punctuation & Grammar Question

5. Rewrite each sentence below, replacing the nouns in bold with their plural.

    a) The books are on the **shelf**. ....

    b) The **chef** made ten **loaf**. ....

    c) **Leaf** fell down on the **roof**. ....

    (3 marks)

Writing Questions

6. Split the extract below into three paragraphs by drawing two lines (//) where each new paragraph should start.

    > One of the girls looks at me in a sharper, more focused way. The look in her eyes isn't curiosity or fear; it's suspicion. "You're new, right?" The voice is cool and deliberate, slightly bored. "I- Yes, that's right," I stutter as the question unsettles me. "I started yesterday."

    (2 marks)

7. Write a short paragraph to continue the story. Think about how to link it to the paragraph directly before, and use descriptive language to make it engaging.

    ....

    ....

    ....

    ....

    ....

    (2 marks)

Score: / 12

Spring Term: Workout 11

Warm up

1. True or false? Texts that inform you about something can be formal or informal.

   ....
   (1 mark)

Reading Questions

A **Wood You Believe That!**

Termites are one of nature's most infamous insects. But despite their minuscule size and problematic appetite for wood, they are actually very impressive creatures. For example, a colony's queen can live for up to 50 years — the longest lifespan of any insect. What's more, termites exhibit characteristics that we humans tend to value: they are able to organise themselves into different roles in their colony and work together to maintain and guard their nest.

B Dear Diary,

I've had a disgusting day. My beautiful house is infested with termites — I'm sure I could hear them chewing my bedroom walls when I woke up this morning. I've called a pest control company to annihilate the beasts, but they can't come until Thursday. In the meantime, I've been doing some research on termites. Did you know there are over 2,700 species of them? Vile. Anyway, I'm off to bed. Goodnight.

2. Tick the boxes to show whether each statement refers to text A, text B or both.

	A	B
The text is about a personal experience with termites.	☐	☐
The text gives factual information about termites.	☐	☐
The text mentions how big termites are.	☐	☐

   (3 marks)

3. Summarise the difference in the writers' attitudes towards termites.

   ....

   ....

   ....
   (2 marks)

Spelling, Punctuation & Grammar Question

4. For each sentence, circle the correct spelling of the word in bold.

   a) The butterfly flapped **it's / its** delicate wings and fluttered into the sky.

   b) **Its / It's** not uncommon for people to hear crickets chirping in their garden.

   c) I just walked past a massive anthill — I bet **it's / its** got a lot of ants inside.

   (3 marks)

Writing Question

5. a) Write a short paragraph that informs the reader about an insect of your choice.

   ....

   ....

   ....
   (1 mark)

   b) Write an explanation of why you like or dislike a different insect of your choice.

   ....

   ....

   ....
   (1 mark)

   c) Write some advice about what you should do if you come across a wasps' nest.

   ....

   ....

   ....
   (1 mark)

   Score: ☐ / 12

Spring Term: Workout 12

Warm up

1. Write down three adjectives that could describe this house.

   ....
   (1 mark)

Reading Questions

> Everything was still. Too still. The rides weren't moving, the music wasn't playing, the lights weren't twinkling. Not even a ripple passed over the pool at the bottom of the water slide. The park was asleep — at least, that's what Sam told himself as he wheeled his cleaning trolley along dark pathways and between dimly lit buildings. The park was merely asleep, innocent under the moonlight. Not dangerous.
>
> But when Sam came to the attraction with life-sized figures, he kept his gaze firmly on the ground, his broom, the walls — anything other than them. The sight of their faces lurking in the darkness never failed to send an uncontrollable shudder down his spine, for though the park was asleep, their eyes were still open.

2. a) Circle the word which best describes the atmosphere created by the setting.

   | pessimistic | despairing | ominous | tranquil |

   b) Find and copy a quote that supports your answer to part a).

   ....

   ....
   (2 marks)

3. a) Which literary device is used in the phrase "The park was asleep"?

   ....

   b) Why do you think the writer uses this literary device throughout the text?

   ....

   ....
   (2 marks)

Spelling, Punctuation & Grammar Question

4. Underline the adverbs in each sentence below.

    a) The books lined the shelves neatly, glinting majestically in the candlelight.

    b) Soon, the volcano will erupt — nearby towns will quickly be covered in ash.

    c) I was quite content to lie in the hammock and watch the clouds drift overhead.

    (3 marks)

Writing Questions

5. Rewrite the text below so that the beach seems relaxing rather than hectic.

    > Children running, screaming, playing; seagulls squawking, flapping, stealing; waves pounding; ice cream melting; sun burning — a day at the beach.

    ....

    ....

    ....
    (1 mark)

6. Write a paragraph to describe one of the settings below. Think about what atmosphere you want to create and how to create it (e.g. vocabulary choice, literary devices).

    | an underwater shipwreck | a cabin in the woods | a sports stadium |

    ....

    ....

    ....

    ....

    ....

    ....
    (3 marks)

    Score: ☐ / 12

Summer Term: Workout 1

Warm up

1. In which text would you be least likely to see a numbered list? Circle your answer.

    a recipe   some instructions   a film review   a to-do list

    (1 mark)

Reading Questions

THE HISTORY OF JOUSTING

What is jousting?
Jousting is a game played on horseback, in which you try to knock your opponent off their horse using a long lance. It is often associated with medieval knights, since many competed in jousting matches.

Where did medieval jousting matches take place?
Most jousting matches took place during specially organised tournaments. Knights would travel from across the land to participate on behalf of their lord.

Did you know?
Some noblemen hired knights to compete for them in tournaments. These knights became known as '**freelancers**', a term that's still used today to refer to people who work for multiple bosses.

2. Why do you think the author has used questions as subheadings?

    ....
    (1 mark)

3. Why do you think the writer arranged the text so that the reader would read the 'Did you know?' box after the other information?

    ....
    (1 mark)

4. Write down one other layout feature used in the text. Explain its effect.

    ....

    ....
    (2 marks)

Spelling, Punctuation & Grammar Question

5. Complete each sentence by circling the correct word in bold.

    a) Knights would **we're / wear / where** heavy armour during jousting matches.

    b) Jousting was sometimes used **too / two / to** prepare knights for war.

    c) King Henry VIII nearly died when he fell **of / off** his horse while jousting.

    (3 marks)

Writing Questions

6. Imagine you are a medieval king hosting a jousting tournament. The plan below is for a speech you will make at the end of the tournament, but the points are in the wrong order. Write the numbers 1-4 in the boxes to put them in the correct order.

    Explain how the winner reached the final and describe the final.

    Explain the plan for next year's tournament and say goodbye.

    Greet everyone and thank them for attending the tournament.

    Announce the tournament winner and describe his background.

    (2 marks)

7. Now imagine you are the tournament winner. Make a short plan for a victory speech to be delivered after the King has finished speaking. Think about how to structure your speech so that you describe your victory but also please the King.

    ....

    ....

    ....

    ....

    ....

    ....

    (2 marks)

Score: ☐ / 12

Summer Term: Workout 2

Warm up

1. Which of these words is **not** spelt correctly? Tick the box.

   criminal ☐   captivitey ☐   sentenced ☐   confinement ☐

   (1 mark)

Reading Questions

> These dungeon walls, they say, have ears,
> And though today the cells lie bare,
> They whisper still of tortured years.
>
> The floors are stained with ancient tears
> Of wretched men in fruitless prayer —
> These dungeon walls, they say, have ears.
>
> Cut off from life among their peers,
> Here men grew desperate in despair,
> As all their hopes turned into fears.
>
> Now when a lone tourist appears,
> They shuffle through, as if aware
> That dungeon walls like these have ears
> And whisper still of tortured years.

2. Find a quote that shows prisoners are no longer kept in the dungeon.

   ....

   (1 mark)

3. The men in the dungeon were "in fruitless prayer". What does this suggest?

   ....

   (1 mark)

4. a) What does the word "shuffle" suggest about how the tourist is walking?

   ....

   b) Why do you think they are walking like this?

   ....

   ....

   (2 marks)

Spelling, Punctuation & Grammar Question

5. Add inverted commas in the correct places to the sentences below.

   a) Don't worry — we'll set you free , she whispered through the bars .

   b) The jailer snarled , Stop complaining or I'll give you no food !

   c) How long have you been here ? the prisoner asked her cellmate .

   (3 marks)

Writing Questions

6. Fill in each gap in the poem below using the simple past tense form of the verb in brackets.

   They .... me to the castle keep, *(to drag)*

   They .... me guilty without trial, *(to find)*

   They .... me into dungeon deep, *(to throw)*

   And .... me rotting in exile. *(to leave)*

   (1 mark)

7. Here is the first line of a different poem. Add three more lines to the poem, using only present tense verbs. Your poem doesn't have to rhyme.

   I sit in darkness in my filthy cell,

   ....

   ....

   ....

   (3 marks)

Score: /12

Summer Term: Workout 3

Warm up

1. If someone mentions a novel's 'context', what are they referring to?

   ....
   (1 mark)

Reading Questions

> My father was a clergyman*, who was deservedly respected by all who knew him. My mother, who married him against the wishes of her friends, was a squire's** daughter, and a woman of spirit. In vain it was represented to her, that if she became the poor parson's* wife, she must give up her carriage and her lady's-maid, and all the luxuries and elegancies of wealth. A carriage and a lady's-maid were great conveniences; but, thank heaven, she had feet to carry her, and hands to take care of her own necessities. An elegant house and spacious grounds were not to be despised; but she would rather live in a cottage with Richard Grey than in a palace with any other man in the world.

*clergyman/parson — *priest*
**squire — *landowner, lord*

An adapted extract from *Agnes Grey* by Anne Brontë

2. What does this extract show about marriage in the mid-nineteenth century?

   ....

   ....
   (1 mark)

3. a) What kind of lifestyle did the narrator's mother have before she was married?

   ....

   b) Find a piece of evidence from the text to support your answer to part a).

   ....

   ....
   (2 marks)

Spelling, Punctuation & Grammar Question

4. Here's another adapted extract from *Agnes Grey*. Underline all 5 adjectives in the text.

   > They seemed bold, lively children, and I hoped I should soon be on friendly terms with them — the little boy especially, of whom I had heard such a favourable character from his mamma.

   (2 marks)

Writing Questions

5. Here is a paragraph from an essay about *Agnes Grey*. Rewrite it, correcting all the spelling, punctuation and grammar mistakes. There are six to spot.

   > As a child, agnes has a high opinian of her father. In Chapter One, she describes him as "deservedly respected by all who knew him. This suggest that Agnes beleives he is worthy of other peoples' respect.

   ....

   ....

   ....

   ....

   (3 marks)

6. Here's another paragraph. Rewrite it, so it uses more interesting language.

   > Agnes's parents have a good relationship. For example, her mother thinks her father is nicer than "any other man in the world". This shows that she really likes him.

   ....

   ....

   ....

   ....

   (3 marks)

Score: /12

Summer Term: Workout 4

> **Warm up**
>
> 1. What is the most likely purpose of emotive language? Tick one option.
>
>   to advise ☐   to explain ☐   to create sympathy ☐   to inform ☐
>
>   *(1 mark)*

Reading Questions

> For thousands of years, humans have been crafting goods and providing services. There is a beauty in a person's ability to work hard, create something useful and exchange it with somebody else. Worryingly, though, this age-old system which has benefitted billions of lives is under threat. According to business leaders in the UK, humanity's usefulness in the workplace is dwindling, with robots set to fill the gaps.
>
> *Not for Bots* is the UK's leading group on preventing a workplace takeover. Already, we have stopped the creation of robots in 300 workplaces, preventing over 2000 job losses, but many others have been unpreventable. We cannot stop this disaster alone.
>
> We need your help. Join the movement today — your job depends on it.

2. How does this text make you feel? Explain your answer.

   ....

   ....
   (2 marks)

3. Which of these is **not** a reason why the writer wrote this text? Tick one option.

   to get people to join *Not for Bots* ☐   to bring attention to job losses ☐

   to praise human workers ☐   to ask people to work harder ☐

   (1 mark)

4. How is this text effective in persuading the reader to join the *Not for Bots* movement? Explain your answer with at least one example.

   ....

   ....
   (2 marks)

Spelling, Punctuation & Grammar Question

5. Fill in the gaps using the conjunctions in the box. Use each conjunction once.

| that | although | as | since |

To reduce fears of a full workplace takeover, some companies have championed 'cobots' .... an alternative to robot-run factories. Cobots are 'collaborative robots', ... they work with humans in a shared workspace. However, ... cobots are designed to alleviate strain, many worry .... they are simply wolves in sheep's clothing.

(2 marks)

Writing Question

6. Write a short text arguing that robots in the workplace are beneficial.
   Use as many persuasive techniques as you can. You could mention how robots:
   - can do repetitive or dangerous jobs
   - work precisely, quickly and efficiently.

....
....
....
....
....
....
....

(4 marks)

Score: /12

Summer Term: Workout 5

Warm up

1. Give one reason a playwright might use stage directions.

   ....
   (1 mark)

Reading Questions

	HERO *swoons*
BEATRICE	Why, how now*, cousin! Wherefore** sink you down?
BENEDICK	How doth the lady?
BEATRICE	Dead, I think. Help, uncle! Hero! Why, Hero! Uncle! Signior Benedick! Friar!
LEONATO	O Fate! Take not away thy heavy hand. Death is the fairest cover for her shame.

At this point in the play, it's Hero's wedding day, but she has just been wrongly accused of having an affair.

*how now — *what's the meaning of this?*
**wherefore — *why*

An abridged extract from *Much Ado About Nothing* by William Shakespeare

2. What happens to Hero at the beginning of the extract?

   ....
   (1 mark)

3. a) Which of the following best describes how Beatrice feels? Tick a box.

   argumentative ☐   gloomy ☐   distressed ☐

   b) Suggest how an actress playing Beatrice could speak and move to show this.

   ....

   ....
   (2 marks)

4. Write down a quote that suggests Leonato believes Hero is guilty.

   ....
   (1 mark)

Spelling, Punctuation & Grammar Question

5. For each sentence, circle the correct spelling of the word in bold.

   a) **Let's / Lets** rehearse the wedding scene again.

   b) We hope the set designer **let's / lets** us use the new props.

   c) Our theatre director never **let's / lets** on when she's impressed.

(3 marks)

Writing Question

6. Here is a modern translation of the next part of *Much Ado About Nothing*. Imagine what might happen next and write the next few lines of the script, using dialogue and stage directions.

BEATRICE	How are you doing, Hero?
	HERO *moves*
FRIAR FRANCIS	Take it easy, my lady.
LEONATO	Is she going to dare to open her eyes?
FRIAR FRANCIS	Yes... Why shouldn't she open them?
LEONATO	Why? Well, because she should be ashamed! How can she deny this rumour when she looks so guilty?

   ....

   ....

   ....

   ....

   ....

   ....

   ....

   ....

(4 marks)

Score: / 12

Summer Term: Workout 6

> **Warm up**
>
> 1. How should you end a letter to someone whose name you don't know? Tick a box.
>
>   Best wishes ☐   Yours faithfully ☐   Yours sincerely ☐
>
>   *(1 mark)*

Reading Questions

> I appreciate you reaching out to me directly to voice your concerns about your recent purchase from Picnic Produce Patch. On behalf of the company, I would like to apologise for any inconvenience caused by finding a caterpillar family in your lettuce.
>
> We work hard to ensure that all our products are as fresh as possible, which is why we send them out within hours of being picked. This means they really have come straight from the farm, so we ask customers to wash them before consuming. That being said, I see that this was disappointing, so I have enclosed a voucher for £5 off your next purchase.
>
> We wholeheartedly assure you that we take feedback very seriously, and we remain devoted to offering our customers the most outstanding service possible. Should you require any further assistance, please do not hesitate to contact us.

2. Who do you think is the author's intended audience?

   ....

   (1 mark)

3. a) Which of the following best describes the author's tone? Circle one.

   | light-hearted | apologetic | sarcastic | critical |

   b) Write out a part of the text that supports this.

   ....

   (2 marks)

4. Why do you think the author uses formal language throughout the text?

   ....

   (1 mark)

Spelling, Punctuation & Grammar Question

5. Fill in the gap in each sentence using either 'a', 'an' or 'the'.

   a) Saffron comes from .... species of crocus.

   b) Pansies do very well in .... cold.

   c) Peonies give off such .... exquisite perfume.

(3 marks)

Writing Question

6. Rewrite the sentences below to make them more interesting. You could add in some adjectives and adverbs, or replace some of the words with synonyms.

   Visitors can walk around the quiet gardens.

   ....

   ....

   Planting lots of different coloured flowers gives a nice look.

   ....

   ....

   Growing your own food is cheap and fun.

   ....

   ....

   The grounds are pretty in the sun.

   ....

   ....

(4 marks)

Score: /12

Summer Term: Workout 7

Warm up

1. Draw lines to link each word to its definition.

   describing an object as if it were human — imagery

   a word that sounds like what it's describing — onomatopoeia

   language that creates a picture in the reader's mind — personification

   (2 marks)

Reading Questions

> We delve through history archives,
> For traces of our name,
> Births and deaths and marriages,
> Our endless shimmering chain...
>
> We leaf through photo albums,
> Of those we never met,
> But who live on in our faces,
> The mirrors don't forget...
>
> We note our similarities,
> Resemblances persist,
> Thank those who came before us,
> Without whom we wouldn't exist...
>
> One day, we'll be someone's history,
> Birthmarks of bygone days,
> Our births, our deaths, our marriages,
> Their endless shimmering chain...

2. What technique is "endless shimmering chain" an example of? Tick a box.

   a simile ☐   an oxymoron ☐   a metaphor ☐

   (1 mark)

3. Why do you think the poet uses ellipses at the end of each stanza? Explain your answer.

   ....
   ....
   ....

   (2 marks)

Spelling, Punctuation & Grammar Question

4. Rewrite each sentence below, replacing the nouns in bold with their plural.

   a) We found **box** of **antique**. ....

   b) They held **rich** of all **kind**. ....

   c) We saw **brooch** and **watch**. ....

   d) There were two **pair** of **glass**. ....

   (4 marks)

Writing Question

5. a) Read the line below, which is from a different poem.
      Write the next line of the poem, using a simile.

      Specks of dust floated through the air

      ....

   b) Here's another line from the same poem.
      Write the line that comes after it, using exaggeration.

      My family valuables seemed to be

      ....

   c) Read this line from the same poem.
      Write the next line, using alliteration.

      Sharing stories by the fire

      ....

   (3 marks)

Score: /12

Summer Term: Workout 8

> **Warm up**
>
> 1. Write either 'have' or 'of' to complete this sentence correctly.
>
>   If we lived closer, I would .... visited my friend when she moved.
>
>   *(1 mark)*

Reading Questions

> Mya and Pip had known each other since birth. Their parents met on the maternity ward, and just 8 minutes stopped the girls from sharing a birthday.
>
> As children, they'd play for hours, and were never punctual for dinner. They would pretend to be astronauts or superheroes or wizards, and they had to save the world before they could sit down at the table.
>
> Now, for the first time, they were parting ways to move to separate cities. As Mya lifted her suitcase into the car boot, she felt a pang of sadness at the thought of not being able to pop round to Pip's house after school. She wondered if they would still talk often.
>
> "Try not to worry, Mya," her dad insisted. "Good friends can't be separated by distance." Mya let out a long, deep sigh. She hoped he was right.

2. What do you think is the main theme explored in this extract?

   ....

   (1 mark)

3. What does Mya think could happen to her and Pip's friendship when she moves?

   ....

   ....

   (1 mark)

4. Find a quote that shows Mya's dad's attitude towards her relationship with Pip.

   ....

   (1 mark)

Spelling, Punctuation & Grammar Question

5. Complete the sentences in the extract below using suitable punctuation.

   > Mya presented Pip with a wad of note paper trimmed with gold borders ......
   > "So we can keep in touch," she said. "You didn't think I'd forget, did you ......
   > "It's perfect," Pip squealed. "What a surprise ......

   (3 marks)

Writing Questions

6. Imagine you're writing a story about two friends who wake up in a TV show.

   a) Write the opening sentence of your story.

   ....

   ....
   (1 mark)

   b) Write the closing sentence of your story.

   ....

   ....
   (1 mark)

7. Below are some story prompts. Write a short plan for one of them.

   | An astronaut visits a new planet and befriends an alien. | Two sworn enemies discover they have more in common than they thought. |

   ....

   ....

   ....

   ....

   ....
   (3 marks)

Score: /12

Summer Term: Workout 9

Warm up

1. Fill in the gaps in the paragraph below.
   The first letter of each missing word has been given to you.

   A writer's **t**............... gives the reader an impression about how they are feeling.

   Humour and **i**........................... language often create a light-hearted tone,

   whereas **f**........................... language can create a more serious tone.

   (2 marks)

Reading Question

> Something certainly is rotten in the state of Denmark, and it might just be last night's production of 'Hamlet' at the Green End Theatre. Set, bizarrely, on some kind of futuristic planet where everyone talks as if they're in a primary school nativity play, this production plods agonisingly along until, finally, the characters put each other and the audience out of their misery. The acting can only be described as tragic, and not in the way Shakespeare intended it, while the ridiculous strobe lighting was so blinding that I found myself wondering, "To see, or not to see?" every time a new scene started.

2. a) Which of the following best describes the tone of the text above? Tick one box.

   glum ☐   critical ☐   enthusiastic ☐

   b) Find a piece of evidence in the text to support your answer.

   ....

   c) Explain how this evidence supports your answer to part a).

   ....

   ....

   ....

   (3 marks)

Spelling, Punctuation & Grammar Question

3. For each sentence, circle the correct spelling of the word in bold.

    a) I wouldn't **recommend / reccommend** this play if you don't like violence.

    b) The director took a very **diferent / different** approach to those before her.

    c) The actors looked **embarassed / embarrassed** to be involved in the production.

    d) The producers are due to speak to the press **tomorrow / tommorrow** .

    (4 marks)

Writing Question

4. The sentences below all come from reviews of theatre productions. Rewrite each sentence so that it uses more formal language.

    > The costumes were the coolest I've ever seen, and the set design was dead good.

    ....

    ....

    > The dancers knocked it out of the park, but the singing was totally rubbish.

    ....

    ....

    > I was wowed by the crazy plot, but the props were a bit lame.

    ....

    ....

    (3 marks)

Score: /12

Summer Term: Workout 10

Warm up

1. Here is a list of things to think about when comparing texts. Add **four** more things.

   ......language, mood, ...

   (2 marks)

Reading Questions

A I turned towards the long narrow windows, and there, sure enough, I saw a little girl, dressed all unfit to be out-of-doors on such a bitter night — crying, and beating against the window-panes, as if she wanted to be let in. She seemed to sob and wail, till Miss Rosamond could bear it no longer, and was flying to the door to open it, when, all of a sudden, the great organ pealed out so loud and thundering, it fairly made me tremble.

B The street lights that once brought steady illumination to the road now flickered sporadically, as if sending out a coded warning. Jerome slowly turned in trepidation at the twilit spectacle. Then all light ceased.

A distant street light flashed into life. A shadowy figure stood in its glow. The light snapped off, and then a nearer street lamp switched on, the figure once again beneath it. It was getting closer!

An abridged extract from *The Old Nurse's Story* by Elizabeth Gaskell

2. Find one similarity between these texts. Support your answer with evidence.

   ....

   ....

   ....

   (2 marks)

3. Find one difference between these texts. Support your answer with evidence.

   ....

   ....

   ....

   (2 marks)

Spelling, Punctuation & Grammar Question

4. For each sentence, circle the correct spelling of the word in bold.

   a) Yesterday, she **thought / thaught** she heard a strange noise.

   b) A cool **drought / draught** whistled through the abandoned house.

   (2 marks)

Writing Questions

5. Read this text carefully. Circle each mistake and write the correction above it.

   > "Come on — we need to leave," Nari bellowed, as the old house ached and growned again. "Min, what are you doing! We need to leave right now!
   >
   > I take one last picture and then turned on my heels. Me and Nari sprinted towards the front door. The house seemed to dis-integrate behind us.

   (2 marks)

6. Rewrite this opening to a horror story to make it more interesting.

   > My next-door neighbours seemed very kind. One day, they invited me for dinner. They made a funny-looking stew. They smiled as I swallowed each mouthful. It was then that I noticed they both had a pair of sharp fangs.

   ....

   ....

   ....

   ....

   ....

   ....

   (2 marks)

Score: /12

Summer Term: Workout 11

Warm up

1. Which of the following would most likely be written in a formal style? Tick a box.

   a diary entry ☐   a government report ☐   a magazine advert ☐

   (1 mark)

Reading Questions

> Sink your teeth into these dental tips to protect your teeth from decay, damage and disease:
>
> 1. Watch your sugar! Too much sugar leads to tooth decay. This is because bacteria use the sugar on your teeth to create acid, which eats away at your gnashers. This causes bad breath and, over time, cavities.
>
> 2. Brush your teeth twice a day! Brushing with toothpaste cleans the bacteria-laden plaque from your teeth, preventing damage from occurring.
>
> 3. Visit your dentist! Regular check-ups means a dentist can spot early damage — and they'll do their best to have you walk away with teeth like pearls.

2. Write a suitable title for this text.

   ....
   (1 mark)

3. Find an example of alliteration from the text.
   Why do you think the writer uses alliteration in this example?

   ....

   ....
   (2 marks)

4. Find one simile from the text and explain its meaning.

   ....

   ....
   (2 marks)

Spelling, Punctuation & Grammar Question

5. Fill in each gap with either a colon or a semi-colon.

> The government has explored various ways of reducing the cost of dental treatments, but they each have drawbacks ...... they could increase taxes on sugar ...... they could divert funds from other healthcare services (or any public services) ...... they could advertise to promote brushing ...... or they could reduce the salaries of dentists.

(2 marks)

Writing Question

6. In the UK, most adults have to pay for dental treatment. Imagine you have been asked to write an essay with the title "Should dentistry be free for everyone?".

   a) Write a sentence giving your opinion about the question in the essay title and briefly explain the main reason for your opinion.

   ....

   ....
   (1 mark)

   b) Write an introduction to the essay based on your answer to part a).

   ....

   ....

   ....

   ....

   ....

   ....

   ....
   (3 marks)

Score: ☐ / 12

Summer Term: Workout 12

Warm up

1. What is the name given to a group of lines in a poem?

   ....

   (1 mark)

Reading Questions

> Eyes watch from the hedgerow,
> Set on the cottage's last light.
> The animals wait patiently,
> For the coming of the night.
>
> Out pops a white and fluffy face,
> With floppy ears and big, wide eyes.
> Then two prickly, brown creatures,
> From the brambles do arise.
>
> A fox, fiery-haired and feisty,
> Seeks out the chicken coop.
> Dreaming of rich, golden egg yolk,
> The tiptoeing fox takes a scoop.
>
> The coop erupts into a cacophony,
> Drowning out the still of night,
> The creatures retreat to the hedge,
> As from the cottage comes a light.

2. What is the rhyme scheme of this poem? Tick the correct option.

   ABCA ☐   ABAB ☐   ABAD ☐   ABCB ☐

   (1 mark)

3. Apart from the fox and the chickens, what other animals are described in the poem?

   ....

   (1 mark)

4. Compare the structure of the beginning and the end of the poem.

   a) Write down one way in which they are similar.

   ....

   b) What effect do you think this has?

   ....

   ....

   (2 marks)

Spelling, Punctuation & Grammar Question

5. Rewrite these lines from the poem so they use the present perfect form. The first one has been done for you.

   a) The animals wait patiently

   ....*The animals have waited patiently*..

   b) The tiptoeing fox takes a scoop

   ....

   c) The coop erupts into a cacophony

   ....

   d) The creatures retreat to the hedge

   ....

   (3 marks)

Writing Question

6. Imagine you are the cottage owner from the poem on page 72. Write 8 lines of poetry in the past tense describing what you saw and heard that night.

   You may want to draft your poem on a piece of paper first.

   ....
   ....
   ....
   ....
   ....
   ....
   ....
   ....

   (4 marks)

   Score: /12

Answers

Autumn Term

Workout 1 — pages 2-3

1. capable *(1 mark)*
2. excitement *(1 mark)*
3. E.g. The word "obsessed" suggests that she has a strong desire to fly. *(1 mark)*
4. "soaring like an eagle (high above the ocean)" *(1 mark)*
5. E.g. She is calm and at peace as she feels herself "relax into the seat". *(1 mark for describing how she feels, 1 mark for using a quote to explain your answer)*
6. Monique pressed firmly on the <u>ignision</u> and felt the <u>powerfull</u> throb of the engines as they coughed once and then roared into deafening life. As they settled to a gentle rumble, she felt the <u>rythm</u> of her heart slow to a steady beat. *(1 mark for underlining each word)*
7. Any sensible answer. E.g. Crackling over the radio, the control tower gave a waiting Monique permission to take off. She gently nudged the throttle forwards. The enormous plane started to zoom along the runway. It moved like a deer being chased by a cheetah. Monique was ecstatic that she was about to fly a plane. *(1 mark for making limited changes to make the text more interesting, or 2-3 marks for making more extensive changes by adding imagery and using adjectives and adverbs)*

Workout 2 — pages 4-5

1. fortunate, historical, financial *(1 mark for all correct)*
2. container *(1 mark)*
3. More than 600 years ago *(1 mark)*
4. E.g. An action that is considered normal or done a lot *(1 mark)*
5. E.g. The word 'pygg' sounds like 'pig', so they started making pig-shaped pots because they enjoyed the pun. *(1 mark)*
6. However$_⌃$ the pig is not the only animal associated with money. In Japanese culture$_⌃$ cats are believed to bring prosperity. Many Japanese businesses display a 'Beckoning Cat' statue — a raised right paw attracts money$_⌃$ whereas a raised left paw attracts customers. Beckoning Cats have found their way into cartoons$_⌃$ art and fashion. *(1 mark for each correct comma)*
7. Any sensible answer. E.g. In Chinese culture, people believe that goldfish bring wealth; this belief has existed for many years. It likely originated because the Chinese words for "fish" and "wealth" sound similar. *(1 mark for changing "reckon", 1 mark for changing "donkey's years", 1 mark for changing "cos")*

Workout 3 — pages 6-7

1. rhythm *(1 mark)*
2. E.g. It suggests that the otter moves gracefully. *(1 mark)*
3. gloomy *(1 mark)*
4. E.g. You should be silent and still. *(1 mark)*
5. E.g. The evenings are peaceful. The words "soft", "balmy" and "idly" suggest that there is a relaxed atmosphere. *(1 mark for describing the evenings, 1 mark for using a quote to explain your answer)*
6. You should have underlined: wait, turns, glides, emerges, shimmer, trots, disappears. *(1 mark for 4 to 6 verbs correctly underlined, or 2 marks for all 7 verbs correctly underlined)*
7. Any sensible answers that rhyme. *(1 mark for each rhyming couplet)*

Workout 4 — pages 8-9

1. short story *(1 mark)*
2. A letter. E.g. The text begins "Hi Mara". *(1 mark)*
3. Informal style *(1 mark)*
4. a) Opinion
   b) Opinion
   c) Fact
   (1 mark for each)
5. a) glimpse
   b) environment
   c) autumn
   (1 mark for each)
6. Any sensible answer. *(1 mark for 1-3 relevant points, or 2 marks for 4-5 relevant points. Then 1 mark for numbering any given points in a sensible order.)*

Workout 5 — pages 10-11

1. free verse *(1 mark)*
2. sonnet *(1 mark)*
3. E.g. It suggests the narrator is writing quickly. *(1 mark)*
4. Any sensible answers. E.g. "I cast a smile pagewards in praise." "They nourish my heart, a spiritual prize." *(1 mark for each quote)*
5. a) Pass the flour <u>through</u> a sieve to eliminate any lumps.
   b) Soften the block of butter <u>in</u> the microwave.
   c) All the bakers <u>except</u> Shelley were extremely nervous.
   d) The showstopping cake was created <u>by</u> the master baker.
   (1 mark for each)
6. Any sensible answer. *(1 mark for every two lines that are written in the acrostic form correctly)*

Answers

Workout 6 — pages 12-13

1. slogan *(1 mark)*
2. the same night *(1 mark)*
3. a) False
   b) False
   c) True
   (1 mark for each)
4. a) The drummer (the musician who started the band) uses a variety of instruments to recreate the sound of crashing waves.
   b) There are rumours (largely unconfirmed ones) that a new album is in the works to capitalise on the success of *Poolside Paradise*.
   (1 mark for each sentence)
5. Any sensible answer.
   (1 mark for completing each row of the table)

Workout 7 — pages 14-15

1. E.g. The way that the events of the story are ordered. *(1 mark)*
2. E.g. He is upset. *(1 mark)*
3. a) The <u>narrator</u> has been knocked down by a punch.
   b) The <u>opponent</u> is burly and grimacing.
   c) After getting up, the narrator is feeling <u>determined</u>.
   (1 mark for each)
4. E.g. They are acting on instinct instead of thinking about their actions. *(1 mark)*
5. a) audience
   b) friend
   c) received
   (1 mark for each)
6. Any sensible answer.
   (1 mark for continuing the paragraph in a way that's consistent with the opening sentence, 1 mark for addressing the question prompt, 1 mark for using appropriate techniques to make the text gripping)

Workout 8 — pages 16-17

1. a guide on making lesson plans — a teacher
   a list of school rules — a pupil
   a report on the UK education system — an MP
   (1 mark for 1 correct, 2 marks for all correct)
2. Any sensible answer.
   E.g. Zene's parents *(1 mark)*
3. Formal. E.g. "I am writing to inform you"
   (1 mark for 'formal', 1 mark for an example)
4. a) self-discipline
   b) re-sent
   c) No hyphen
   (1 mark for each)
5. It's a good idea to set aside a few minutes every day to practise. *(1 mark)*
6. Any sensible answer.
   (1 mark for using language to advise, 1 mark for using a letter format, 1 mark for using informal language)

Workout 9 — pages 18-19

1. When summarising a text, you should write down <u>the key points</u>. In a summary, you should use <u>your own words</u>.
   (1 mark for each)
2. Ewan is careless, whereas Alice is cautious. *(1 mark)*
3. Any sensible answer.
   E.g. Ewan and Alice sneak into Gran's attic, but they're surprised by Gran returning home.
   (1 mark for describing Alice and Ewan in the attic, 1 mark for mentioning Gran coming home)
4. a) Alice found <u>it</u>.
   b) <u>They</u> had torches.
   (1 mark for each)
5. Any sensible answers.
   E.g. ALICE *(in a furious whisper)* What have you done? Let's go!
   EWAN There's no time — I can hear her footsteps. We'll just have to hide.
   <u>The children quickly hide behind some large boxes.</u>
   (1 mark for each)
6. Any sensible answer.
   (1 mark for dialogue that shows Gran discovering Alice and Ewan, 1 mark for setting out the speakers and dialogue correctly, 1 mark for using stage directions)

Workout 10 — pages 20-21

1. a newspaper article about a famous climber — to inform
   a children's story about a magical journey — to entertain
   a magazine article with tips for buying walking boots — to advise
   (1 mark for 1 correct, or 2 marks for all correct)
2. to persuade *(1 mark)*
3. Any sensible answer.
   E.g. The writer's exaggerated promise to turn the reader's "dream into a reality" aims to persuade the reader that going on a trek is an unmissable experience.
   (1 mark for an appropriate piece of evidence, 1 mark for an explanation)
4. a) The trail is <u>busier</u> in summer than in winter.
   b) New Zealand is even <u>more beautiful</u> than I expected.
   c) The west coast has <u>wetter</u> weather than the east.
   (1 mark for each)
5. a) Any sensible answers.
   E.g. <u>In addition</u>, mountaineering gives people…
   <u>However</u>, few people realise…
   (1 mark for each)
   b) Any sensible answer.
   (1 mark for writing two sentences which justify starting a new paragraph, 1 mark for using an appropriate linking word)

Answers

Workout 11 — pages 22-23

1. E.g. The pattern of rhymes at the end of a poem's lines. *(1 mark)*

2. E.g. He is looking intently without looking away. *(1 mark)*

3. E.g. "What a loser!" *(1 mark)*

4. Any sensible answer.
E.g. The passer-by spends her free time waiting for a TV programme. This is similar to the trainspotter waiting for a train.
(1 mark for describing the passer-by, 1 mark for linking the passer-by to the trainspotter)

5. <u>O</u>n <u>F</u>riday, <u>I</u> took the train to <u>Y</u>ork to see my friend <u>A</u>my. <u>S</u>adly, it was delayed.
(1 mark for every 2 capital letters added in the correct place)

6. a) Any sensible answers.
(1 mark for a list of relevant words and phrases)
b) Any sensible answer that includes a verse made up of rhyming couplets.
(1 mark for each line of verse which forms part of a rhyming couplet)

Workout 12 — pages 24-25

1. True *(1 mark)*

2. a) like a crocodile (emerging from a swamp)
b) splash
(1 mark for each)

3. a) personification (or metaphor)
b) menacing
(1 mark for each)

4. You should have underlined: excitement, freedom, feeling, mysteries
(1 mark for every 2 correct)

5. Any sensible answers.
a) E.g. Aisyah was a <u>glistening fish</u> in the water.
b) E.g. The waves were <u>reckless bulls</u> as they crashed into the shore.
(1 mark for each)

6. Any sensible answer that describes what the island is like.
(1 mark for using appropriate descriptive language for the island, 1 mark for including a simile, 1 mark for including a metaphor)

Spring Term

Workout 1 — pages 26-27

1. You should have underlined: Enter, fasten, start *(1 mark for all)*

2. E.g. To make it easier for the reader to find information. *(1 mark)*

3. E.g. It shows how big Mini-Earth is compared to Earth. *(1 mark)*

4. E.g. To introduce the reader to how Mini-Earth was found before going into more specific detail about the planet.
(1 mark)

5. a) The scientists gave us <u>advice</u> about travelling to outer space.
b) Before going to space, you should <u>practise</u> being in zero gravity.
c) The astronaut recently acquired their <u>licence</u> to fly a spacecraft.
(1 mark for each)

6. Any sensible answers.
(1 mark for each step)

7. Any sensible answers.
(1 mark for addressing the paragraph to astronauts, 1 mark for giving information about Mini-Earth's climate, 1 mark for giving advice on what to bring)

Workout 2 — pages 28-29

1. False. *(1 mark)*

2. confident *(1 mark)*

3. E.g. That she tries to appear friendly when she speaks.
(1 mark)

4. E.g. The figure opens the door "only a sliver", which suggests they are trying to hide something from Inspector Ricci's sight.
(1 mark for a relevant quote, 1 mark for an explanation)

5. a) Yes
b) No
c) No
(1 mark for each)

6. Any sensible answer.
(1 mark for writing a version which is clearly based on the original text, 1 mark for showing the character is nervous through what they say, 1 mark for showing the character is nervous through their behaviour, 1 mark for including an effective comparison that shows they are nervous)

Workout 3 — pages 30-31

1. those *(1 mark)*

2. Any sensible answers.
a) E.g. What Pedro did during the summer.
b) E.g. Dangers faced by sea turtles.
(1 mark for each)

3. E.g. He found the work rewarding but also tiring. *(1 mark)*

4. E.g. "taking action does make a difference" *(1 mark)*

5. a) picked / threw
b) got / took
(1 mark for each sentence)

Answers

6. Wow, your trip sounds <u>amazing</u>!
I had a similar experience this summer, actually. I <u>decided</u> to volunteer at my local animal shelter, where I helped <u>to</u> take care of many creatures. The <u>kittens</u> were particularly adorable. However, the lizard (which was very irritable<u>)</u>, kept scratching me. My kindness didn't seem to <u>affect</u> its mood, but I still tried.
(1 mark for every two mistakes corrected)

7. Any sensible answer.
E.g. A sea turtle, upon hatching, ventures out into the sea. With impressive navigating skills, it is then able to locate the area where it was born in order to return and lay its eggs. Once matured, these offspring return to this same beach to lay their own eggs, repeating the cycle.
(1 mark for using more interesting vocabulary, 1 mark for using more interesting sentence structures)

Workout 4 — pages 32-33

1. the text's main idea *(1 mark)*

2. a) They are used to being in a kayak.
   b) Any sensible answer.
   E.g. The narrator says they are "one" with the kayak.
   (1 mark for each)

3. Any sensible quote.
   E.g. Dragging me into the torrent.
   (1 mark)

4. Any sensible answer.
   E.g. Nature is more powerful, as the paddle is described as a "dead weight", suggesting the narrator is powerless to resist the river's pull.
   (1 mark)

5. a) I <u>toss</u> like a leaf in a gale.
   b) Panic nearly <u>consumes</u> me.
   c) The jagged rock <u>approaches</u> too fast.
   (1 mark for each)

6. Any sensible answers.
   E.g. I paddle like an Olympian and narrowly miss the jagged rock.
   I am mercifully carried out of the rumbling rapids.
   I float downstream like a leaf swirling in the current.
   The water is a smooth mirror now.
   (1 mark for each)

Workout 5 — pages 34-35

1. E.g. In time order *(1 mark)*

2. E.g. In the second paragraph, the story goes back in time to describe what happened in the match. *(1 mark)*

3. E.g. It suggests they were nervous. *(1 mark)*

4. a) E.g. Because they were so shocked after scoring the winning goal that they couldn't speak.
   b) E.g. "I was dumbstruck"
   (1 mark for each)

5. a) Kwame rapidly ran <u>past</u> the defender.
   b) Everyone <u>except</u> the goalkeeper was in the box.
   c) <u>There</u> was not much time until the final whistle.
   (1 mark for each)

6. a) Any sensible answer.
   (1 mark for a plan based on one of the topics, 1 mark for planning the opening, middle and ending)
   b) Any sensible answer.
   (1 mark for a sensible opening based on the plan from part a), 1 mark for a clear attempt to engage the reader's interest)

Workout 6 — pages 36-37

1. E.g. An autobiography is written by the person it's about, whereas a biography is written by somebody else. *(1 mark)*

2. It's written in first-person narration because it uses 'I'. *(1 mark)*

3. E.g. "each one wanting to be rid of the Romans" *(1 mark)*

4. It is in inverted commas.
   E.g. This suggests that the writer doesn't actually believe the people had accepted Roman rule.
   (1 mark for 'inverted commas', 1 mark for a sensible explanation)

5. a) I am not <u>hopeful</u> that we will win this battle.
   b) I could hear the Romans marching <u>steadily</u>.
   c) Then, the marching stopped. It was <u>strangely</u> quiet.
   (1 mark for each)

6. Any sensible answer.
   E.g. The British people's resistance to Roman rule took place over several decades and involved many key figures. Warrior Caratacus, and years later, Boudica, both fought the Romans in battle. Further north, the Scottish Picts also made life difficult for their Roman occupiers, causing the Romans to begin building Hadrian's Wall in defence.
   (1 mark for introducing the essay topic, 1 mark for mentioning each of the three points in the mind map)

Workout 7 — pages 38-39

1. E.g. A long speech given by a single character. *(1 mark)*

2. E.g. She speaks "eagerly" when asking for a taste. *(1 mark)*

3. E.g. She doesn't want Hilda to hear what she's saying. *(1 mark)*

4. E.g. No, because Hilda knocks it over "accidentally" and Aggie doesn't say anything before leaving the room.
   (1 mark for giving an opinion, 1 mark for giving relevant evidence from the text)

5. a) Chop an onion, a rat's tail, a hemlock root and a piece of bark.
   b) Take the lock of hair, tie it into a knot and dip it in the liquid.
   c) Mix in the soot, stir once, drop in a frog's leg and let it simmer.
   (1 mark for each sentence)

Answers

6. Any sensible answer.
   E.g. AGGIE *and* HILDA *are in a richly-decorated palace with large portraits on the walls.* AGGIE *is clutching a small glass bottle under her long black cloak. The* PRINCE *approaches them cautiously.*
   PRINCE And so we meet again... *(hushed)* Have you cooked up your marvellous concoction?
   AGGIE Of course. *(AGGIE produces the inky potion)* It's our strongest one yet.
   PRINCE *(He suddenly grabs the potion and drinks it in one noisy gulp.)* Ew! That tastes like a mouldy turnip!
   (1 mark for making the initial stage directions more interesting, 1 mark for each line of speech that is made more interesting)

Workout 8 — pages 40-41

1. to persuade *(1 mark)*

2. Be at one with nature. *(1 mark)*

3. a) command
   b) superlative
   c) rhetorical question
   d) simile
   (1 mark for each)

4. a) Have you experienced a Sheepsdale Campsite bed yet?
   b) There are some breathtaking views at Planter's Gorge.
   c) "Sheepsdale is unbelievable," one customer said. "What a holiday!"
   (1 mark for each)

5. Any sensible answer that uses a list of three.
   E.g. The AlwaysBright torch is durable, lightweight and extremely long-lasting.
   (1 mark)

6. Any sensible answer.
   (1 mark for an advert that gives information about the equipment, 1 mark for using appropriate persuasive techniques)

Workout 9 — pages 42-43

1. Second-person (narration) *(1 mark)*

2. A house *(1 mark)*

3. You should have circled: so the reader can understand the narrator's feelings
   (1 mark)

4. a) E.g. gloomy
   (1 mark)
   b) E.g. bare, stagnant, empty
   (1 mark for 3 sensible words)

5. You should have underlined: weather, piece, here, maybe
   (1 mark for each)

6. Any sensible pair of lines that rhyme and have an excited tone.
   (1 mark)

7. Any sensible answer.
   (1 mark for four lines that continue the poem, 1 mark for using a consistent tone)

Workout 10 — pages 44-45

1. Any sensible answer.
   E.g. A different person is being described, the setting changes, the time changes, the topic changes
   (1 mark)

2. Any sensible answers.
   E.g. concerned, intrigued, sympathetic
   (1 mark for three words)

3. Any sensible answer.
   E.g. It makes it easier for the reader to empathise with the narrator.
   (1 mark)

4. a) frustrated
   b) Any sensible explanation.
   E.g. The narrator says "whatever that means", which suggests they are frustrated because they don't understand why they don't fit in.
   (1 mark for each)

5. a) The books are on the <u>shelves</u>.
   b) The <u>chefs</u> made ten <u>loaves</u>.
   c) <u>Leaves</u> fell down on the <u>roofs</u>.
   (1 mark for each sentence)

6. One of the girls looks at me in a sharper, more focused way. The look in her eyes isn't curiosity or fear; it's suspicion. // "You're new, right?" The voice is cool and deliberate, slightly bored. // "I- Yes, that's right," I stutter as the question unsettles me. "I started yesterday."
   (1 mark for each paragraph break)

7. Any sensible answer.
   (1 mark for continuing the story from the previous paragraph, 1 mark for using descriptive language to make the text engaging)

Workout 11 — pages 46-47

1. True *(1 mark)*

2. The text is about a personal experience with termites. — B
   The text gives factual information about termites. — A and B
   The text mentions how big termites are. — A
   (1 mark for each)

3. E.g. The writer of Text A thinks termites are interesting creatures, whereas the writer of Text B sees termites as an unwanted pest.
   (1 mark for summarising each opinion)

4. a) The butterfly flapped <u>its</u> delicate wings and fluttered into the sky.
   b) <u>It's</u> not uncommon for people to hear crickets chirping in their garden.
   c) I just walked past a massive anthill — I bet <u>it's</u> got a lot of ants inside.
   (1 mark for each)

Answers

5. a) Any sensible answer.
    (1 mark for giving factual information to inform the reader)
    b) Any sensible answer.
    (1 mark for giving at least one reason as to why you like or dislike the insect)
    c) Any sensible answer.
    (1 mark for making suggestions to the reader about what they should do)

Workout 12 — pages 48-49

1. E.g. damaged, large, haunted
    (1 mark for 3 sensible adjectives)
2. a) ominous
    b) E.g. "Everything was still. Too still."
    (1 mark for each)
3. a) personification
    b) E.g. It makes the park seem alive which adds to the sense of fear.
    (1 mark for each)
4. a) The books lined the shelves neatly, glinting majestically in the moonlight.
    b) Soon, the volcano will erupt — nearby towns will quickly be covered in ash.
    c) I was quite content to lie in the hammock and watch the clouds drift overhead.
    (1 mark for each sentence)
5. Any sensible answer.
    E.g. All around, children chuckle happily as the gulls caw softly overhead. The tide rolls idly as people clutch ice cream cones that slowly drip in the cheerful sunshine — a day at the beach.
    (1 mark)
6. Any sensible answer.
    (1 mark for describing one of the settings given, 1 mark for using interesting vocabulary, 1 mark for giving your setting a particular atmosphere)

Summer Term

Workout 1 — pages 50-51

1. a film review *(1 mark)*
2. E.g. It makes the text seem like a conversation between the reader asking questions and the writer answering them. *(1 mark)*
3. E.g. To fully understand the text in the box, you need to have read the other information first. *(1 mark)*
4. E.g. A heading. It catches the reader's attention and tells them what the text is about.
    (1 mark for identifying a layout feature, 1 mark for explaining its effect)
5. a) Knights would wear heavy armour during jousting matches.
    b) Jousting was sometimes used to prepare knights for war.
    c) King Henry VIII nearly died when he fell off his horse while jousting.
    (1 mark for each)
6. 1 — Greet everyone and thank them for attending the tournament.
    2 — Announce the tournament winner and describe his background.
    3 — Explain how the winner reached the final and describe the final.
    4 — Explain the plan for next year's tournament and say goodbye.
    (1 mark for 2 correct, or 2 marks for all correct)
7. Any sensible answer.
    (1 mark for structuring your plan into points or paragraphs, 1 mark for addressing the question prompt)

Workout 2 — pages 52-53

1. captivitey *(1 mark — it should be spelt captivity)*
2. E.g. "today the cells lie bare". *(1 mark)*
3. E.g. They had no hope of leaving the dungeon. *(1 mark)*
4. a) E.g. They are walking slowly and quietly.
    b) E.g. They are aware of all the prisoners who once suffered in the dungeon.
    (1 mark for each)
5. a) "Don't worry — we'll set you free," she whispered through the bars.
    b) The jailer snarled, "Stop complaining or I'll give you no food!"
    c) "How long have you been here?" the prisoner asked her cellmate.
    (1 mark for each sentence)
6. They dragged me to the castle keep,
    They found me guilty without trial,
    They threw me into dungeon deep,
    And left me rotting in exile.
    (1 mark for all)
7. Any sensible answer that uses only present tense verbs.
    (1 mark for each line)

Workout 3 — pages 54-55

1. E.g. Where and when a text was written *(1 mark)*
2. Any sensible answer.
    E.g. It was frowned upon for rich women to marry poorer men.
    (1 mark)
3. a) E.g. She had a luxurious lifestyle.
    b) E.g. "all the luxuries and elegancies of wealth"
    (1 mark for each)

Answers

4. You should have underlined: bold, lively, friendly, little, favourable
   (1 mark for 3-4 adjectives correctly underlined, or 2 marks for all 5 adjectives correctly underlined)

5. As a child, <u>Agnes</u> has a high <u>opinion</u> of her father. In Chapter One, she describes him as "deservedly respected by all who knew him<u>."</u> This <u>suggests</u> that Agnes <u>believes</u> he is worthy of other <u>people's</u> respect.
   (1 mark for every 2 corrections)

6. Any sensible answer.
   E.g. Agnes's parents have a close and loving relationship. For example, her mother thinks her father is more wonderful than "any other man in the world." This shows the strength of her affection for him.
   (1 mark for rewriting each sentence)

Workout 4 — pages 56-57

1. to create sympathy *(1 mark)*

2. Any sensible answer.
   E.g. Worried, because the text says that many people are losing their jobs to robots.
   (1 mark for describing how the text makes you feel, 1 mark for giving an explanation)

3. to ask people to work harder *(1 mark)*

4. Any sensible answer.
   (1 mark for giving a reason the text is effective, 1 mark for explaining with an example)

5. To reduce fears of a full workplace takeover, some companies have championed 'cobots' <u>as</u> an alternative to robot-run factories. Cobots are 'collaborative robots', <u>since</u> they work with humans in a shared workspace. However, <u>although</u> cobots are designed to alleviate strain, many worry <u>that</u> they are simply wolves in sheep's clothing.
   (1 mark for every two correct answers)

6. Any sensible answer.
   (1 mark for a simple description of workplace robots, or 2-3 marks for a short text which explains some of the benefits of workplace robots but with limited use of persuasive techniques, or 4 marks for a detailed text which argues convincingly for the use of workplace robots using a variety of persuasive techniques)

Workout 5 — pages 58-59

1. E.g. to tell the actors when to enter and exit *(1 mark)*

2. Any sensible answer.
   E.g. She faints. *(1 mark)*

3. a) distressed
   b) E.g. She could stutter her lines and pace around the stage.
   (1 mark for each)

4. E.g. "Death is the fairest cover for her shame."
   (1 mark)

5. a) <u>Let's</u> rehearse the wedding scene again.
   b) We hope the set designer <u>lets</u> us use the new props.
   c) Our theatre director never <u>lets</u> on when she's impressed.
   (1 mark for each)

6. Any sensible answer.
   (2 marks for continuing the play in a sensible way, 1 mark for setting out the dialogue correctly, 1 mark for using stage directions correctly)

Workout 6 — pages 60-61

1. Yours faithfully *(1 mark)*

2. E.g. Someone who has sent the company a letter of complaint.
   (1 mark)

3. a) apologetic
   b) E.g. "I would like to apologise for any inconvenience caused"
   (1 mark for each)

4. E.g. To show that the company is professional. *(1 mark)*

5. a) Saffron comes from <u>a</u> species of crocus.
   b) Pansies do very well in <u>the</u> cold.
   c) Peonies give off such <u>an</u> exquisite perfume.
   (1 mark for each)

6. Any sensible answers.
   E.g. Visitors can amble around the tranquil gardens.
   Planting an explosion of different coloured flowers creates an attractive appearance.
   Cultivating your own produce is inexpensive and enjoyable.
   The vast grounds stretch out beautifully in the warm sun.
   (1 mark for each)

Workout 7 — pages 62-63

1. describing an object as if it were human — personification
   a word that sounds like what it's describing — onomatopoeia
   language that creates a picture in the reader's mind — imagery
   (1 mark for one correct, or 2 marks for all correct)

2. a metaphor *(1 mark)*

3. E.g. Each ellipsis creates a pause, which symbolises the passing of time.
   (1 mark for explaining that ellipses create a pause, 1 mark for describing the effect of this)

4. a) We found <u>boxes</u> of <u>antiques</u>.
   b) They held <u>riches</u> of all <u>kinds</u>.
   c) We saw <u>brooches</u> and <u>watches</u>.
   d) There were two <u>pairs</u> of <u>glasses</u>.
   (1 mark for each sentence)

5. a) E.g. Like smoke rising from a cauldron
   b) E.g. Older than time itself
   c) E.g. Funny folk tales and mesmerising myths
   (1 mark for each)

Answers

Workout 8 — pages 64-65

1. have *(1 mark)*

2. Any sensible answer. E.g. friendship *(1 mark)*

3. E.g. She is worried that she and Pip will drift apart. *(1 mark)*

4. E.g. "Good friends can't be separated by distance." *(1 mark)*

5. Mya presented Pip with a wad of note paper trimmed with gold borders. "So we can keep in touch," she said. "You didn't think I'd forget, did you?" "It's perfect," Pip squealed. "What a surprise!"
(1 mark for each sentence)

6. a) Any sensible opening sentence that matches the story prompt. *(1 mark)*
   b) Any sensible closing sentence that matches the story prompt. *(1 mark)*

7. Any sensible answer.
(1 mark for planning the beginning of the story, 1 mark for planning the middle, 1 mark for planning the end)

Workout 9 — pages 66-67

1. A writer's tone gives the reader an impression about how they are feeling. Humour and informal language often create a light-hearted tone, whereas formal language can create a more serious tone.
(1 mark for 2 correct, or 2 marks for all correct)

2. a) critical
   b) E.g. "this production plods agonisingly along"
   c) E.g. This suggests that the author is critical of the play because it isn't gripping, so it's not enjoyable to watch.
(1 mark for each)

3. a) I wouldn't recommend this play if you don't like violence.
   b) The director took a very different approach to those before her.
   c) The actors looked embarrassed to be involved in the production.
   d) The producers are due to speak to the press tomorrow.
(1 mark for each)

4. Any sensible answers.
E.g. The costumes were excellent, and the set design was outstanding. The dancers were extremely talented, but the standard of the singing could have been higher. I found the plot enthralling, but the props were disappointing.
(1 mark for each sentence)

Workout 10 — pages 68-69

1. Any sensible answers.
E.g. audience, purpose, layout, setting, perspective, structure, themes, genre.
(1 mark for every two items added to the list)

2. Any sensible answer.
E.g. Both texts are set at night. Text A is set on a "bitter night" and in Text B there is a "twilit spectacle".
(1 mark for a valid similarity, 1 mark for giving evidence)

3. Any sensible answer.
E.g. Text A is written in the first person, e.g. "I turned", whereas Text B is written in the third person, e.g "Jerome slowly turned".
(1 mark for a valid difference, 1 mark for giving evidence)

4. a) Yesterday, she thought she heard a strange noise.
   b) A cool draught whistled through the abandoned house.
(1 mark for each)

5. "Come on — we need to leave," Nari bellowed, as the old house ached and groaned again. "Min, what are you doing? We need to leave right now!" I took one last picture and then turned on my heels. Nari and I sprinted towards the front door. The house seemed to disintegrate behind us.
(1 mark for 3-5 correct, or 2 marks for all correct)

6. Any sensible answer.
E.g. My elderly next-door neighbours seemed friendly. One winter's evening, they invited me for a home-cooked dinner. They rustled up an unusual-looking colourful stew. They grinned unnervingly as I self-consciously swallowed each mouthful. It was then that I realised, with a flash of horror, that they both had a glistening pair of razor-sharp fangs.
(1 mark for retelling the story, 1 mark for using interesting vocabulary and sentence structures)

Workout 11 — pages 70-71

1. a government report *(1 mark)*

2. Any sensible answer.
E.g. Three Tips for Looking After Your Teeth
(1 mark)

3. decay, damage and disease.
E.g. It emphasises the negative impact of the words, which makes the reader want to read on to find out how to prevent them.
(1 mark for an example of alliteration, 1 mark for a suitable explanation)

4. walk away with teeth like pearls
E.g. It means that the teeth are as shiny and white as pearls.
(1 mark for the simile, 1 mark for a suitable explanation)

Answers

5. The government has explored various ways of reducing the cost of dental treatments, but they each have drawbacks: they could increase taxes on sugar; they could divert funds from other healthcare services (or any public services); they could advertise to promote brushing; or they could reduce the salaries of dentists.
    (1 mark for every two correct answers)

6. a) Any sensible answer.
       (1 mark for an opinion with a suitable explanation)
    b) Any sensible answer.
       (1 mark for introducing the topic and giving your opinion, 1 mark for outlining the reasons for your opinion, 1 mark for using an appropriate formal style)

6. Any sensible answer.
    (1 mark for describing the same events as in the original poem, 1 mark for writing from the cottage owner's perspective, 1 mark for using the past tense, 1 mark for making your poem 8 lines long)

Workout 12 — pages 72-73

1. a verse (or a stanza)
    (1 mark)

2. ABCB *(1 mark)*

3. Any convincing answer based on the evidence in the poem.
    E.g. a rabbit and two hedgehogs
    (1 mark)

4. a) Any suitable answer.
       E.g. In both stanzas, the rhyming words are 'light' and 'night'.
    b) Any answer.
       E.g. The repeated rhyme represents the repeated cycle of the light turning off and then going back on again.
    (1 mark for each)

5. b) The tiptoeing fox <u>has taken</u> a scoop
    c) The coop <u>has erupted</u> into a cacophony
    d) The creatures <u>have retreated</u> to the hedge
    (1 mark for each)

Glossary

alliteration	When words that are close together start with the same sound. E.g. "a big blue bag"
audience	The person or group of people who read or listen to a text or watch a play.
context	The background to a text which affects the way the text is understood.
dialogue	A conversation between two or more people in a play or novel.
figurative language	Language that is used in a non-literal way to create an effect, e.g. personification.
hyperbole	When exaggeration is used to have an effect on the reader.
imagery	Language that creates a picture in your mind, e.g. metaphors and similes.
inference	Reaching an idea or conclusion, based on evidence.
list of three	Using three words (often adjectives) or phrases together to create emphasis.
metaphor	A way of describing something by saying that it is something else.
mood	The general feel or atmosphere of a text, e.g. humorous, peaceful, fearful.
narrative	Writing that tells a story or describes an experience.
narrator	The voice or character speaking the words of the narrative.
onomatopoeia	A word that imitates the sound it describes, e.g. "crunch".
personification	Describing a non-living thing as if it's a person. E.g. "The moon smiled at us."
purpose	The reason someone writes a text, e.g. to persuade, to argue, to advise, to inform.
rhetorical question	A question that doesn't need an answer but is asked to emphasise a point.
rhyming couplet	A pair of rhyming lines that are next to each other.
rhythm	A pattern of sounds created by the arrangement of syllables.
simile	A way of describing something by saying it is like something else.
stage directions	Written instructions in a play that describe how the play should be performed.
stanza	A group of lines in a poem, also known as a verse.
structure	The order and arrangement of ideas in a text. E.g. How it begins, develops and ends.
theme	A recurring idea in a play, novel or poem.
tone	The feeling created by the language of a piece of writing, e.g. happy, sad, serious.

Score Sheet

Fill in the score sheet after you finish each workout.

Write your scores below to show how you've done.
Each workout is out of 12 marks.

	Autumn Term	Spring Term	Summer Term
Workout 1			
Workout 2			
Workout 3			
Workout 4			
Workout 5			
Workout 6			
Workout 7			
Workout 8			
Workout 9			
Workout 10			
Workout 11			
Workout 12			